5/4/11
7003/6578
£14.99

Bryony Lavery

Plays: 1

Origin of the Species, Two Marias, Her Aching Heart, Nothing Compares to You

'In Bryony Lavery's quirky *Origin of the Species*, an ardent archaeologist digging for prehistoric man finds instead a four-million-year-old woman . . . The crunch comes when the "child" has to learn about cruelty and war, in a gentle but telling allegory of the loss of innocence . . . Lavery's wit and imagination are unquestionably present . . . immensely enjoyable.' *Observer*

Lyrical and poignant, *Two Marias* is set in Andalucia, Spain, and explores family identity, love, death and faith.

Her Aching Heart: 'A deliciously irreverent parody of the historical romance, better known as the bonk-buster . . . Georgette Heyer never wrote anything quite like it, however, and Barbara Cartland would be more than confused by this lesbian romance . . . hilarious.' *Guardian*
'A clever and funny, honest and wise comedy on the errors and terrors of love.' *Glasgow Herald*
'Bryony Lavery hits the spot with her hysterical, historical romance . . . I never knew sexual politics could be this much fun.' *Time Out*

Nothing Compares to You: 'Bryony Lavery's play not only shares a title with Sinead O'Connor's poignant hit single, but a focus upon the powerful emotions of loss, grief and desire . . . The characters may be touched by death but laughter is never far away . . . A haunting show of hidden depth.' *Birmingham Post*

Bryony Lavery's plays include *Helen and Her Friends* (1978), *Bag* (1979), *Family Album* (1980), *Missing* (1981), *Calamity* (1983), *Origin of the Species* (1984), *Witchcraze* (1985), *Her Aching Heart* (1990, *Pink Paper* Play of the Year 1991), *Wicked* (1990), *Kitchen Matters* (1990), *Flight* (1991), *Nothing Compares to You* (1995), *Ophelia* (1996) and *Frozen* (1997). For five years she was Artistic Director of Les Ouefs Malades. She was joint Artistic Director of Gay Sweatshop from 1989 to 1991 and a Tutor in Playwriting on the MA Playwriting course at Birmingham University for three years. She was Resident Playwright at the Unicorn Theatre for Children, 1986–7, and her work for children includes *The Zulu Hut Club* (1983), *Sore Points* (1985), *Madagascar* (1987), *The Dragon Wakes* (1988), and *Down Among the Mini-Beasts* (1996) which was nominated for Best Children's Play Writers Guild Awards 1996. Her cabaret work includes *Time Gentlemen Please* (1978), *Female Trouble* (1981), *More Female Trouble* (1982), *The Wandsworth Warmers* (1984). She has appeared in the first five legendary Drill Hall pantomimes and co-written two of them, *Peter Pan* (1991) and *The Sleeping Beauty* (1992).

BRYONY LAVERY

Plays: 1

Origin of the Species
Two Marias
Her Aching Heart
Nothing Compares to You

introduced by the author

Methuen Drama

METHUEN DRAMA CONTEMPORARY DRAMATISTS

This edition first published in Great Britain in 1998
by Methuen Drama

Origin of the Species first published in *Plays by Women* vol. 6
in 1987, by Methuen London Ltd
Copyright © 1987 Bryony Lavery
Two Marias and *Her Aching Heart* first published in a volume together in
1991 by Methuen Drama
Two Marias copyright © 1991 Bryony Lavery
Her Aching Heart copyright © Bryony Lavery
Nothing Compares to You first published in this edition
Copyright © 1998 Bryony Lavery
Collection and Introduction copyright © 1998 Bryony Lavery
The author has asserted her rights under the Copyright,
Designs and Patents Act 1988 to be identified as the author of these works

ISBN 0 413 72340 2

A CIP catalogue record for this book is available at the British Library.

Typeset by Deltatype Ltd, Birkenhead, Merseyside
Transferred to digital printing 2002.

Caution

Contents

Bryony Lavery
A Chronology

1976   *I Was Too Young At The Time To Understand Why My Mother Was Crying/Sharing*, Les Oeufs Malades, Drill Hall, London

1977   *Grandmother's Footsteps*, Les Oeufs Malades, King's Head Theatre, London
Floorshow (cabaret with Caryl Churchill, Micheline Wandor and David Bradford), Monstrous Regiment, national tour
The Catering Service, Les Oeufs Malades, national tour

1978   *Time Gentlemen Please* (cabaret), Monstrous Regiment, national tour
Helen and Her Friends, Les Oeufs Malades, King's Head

1979   *Gentlemen Prefer Blondes*, Monstrous Regiment, national tour
The Wild Bunch (for children), Women's Theatre Group, national tour
Bag, Les Oeufs Malades, national tour

1980   *Zulu* (with Patrick Barlow), The National Theatre of Brent, ICA, London, and national tour
Family Album, Les Oeufs Malades, ICA and national tour

1981   *Female Trouble* (cabaret), Arts Theatre, London
Missing, Extraordinary Productions, national tour
Revolting Women (for television)

1982   *More Female Trouble* (cabaret), Edinburgh Festival and national tour
The Black Hole of Calcutta (with Patrick Barlow), The National Theatre of Brent, University Theatre, Colchester, and national tour
Götterdämmerung (with Patrick Barlow and Susan Todd), The National Theatre of Brent, Edinburgh Festival and national tour

Introduction

The four plays in this volume have a characteristic in common. I was commissioned to write one thing, and I blithely wrote something else. It is to the considerable credit of the four companies who employed me to write these four pieces that they generously came along with me on a journey whose destination was far in the distance, at the back of my head.

In 1844, evolutionist Robert Chambers conceived the following metaphor for the study of evolution:

> Suppose that a mayfly, hovering over a pool for its one April day of life, were capable of observing the fry of the frog in the waters below. In its aged afternoon, having seen no change upon them for such a long time, it would be little qualified to conceive that the external branchiae of these creatures were to decay, and be replaced by internal lungs, that feet were to be developed, the tail erased, and the animal then to become a denizen of the land.

This is my only defence. As a playwright, I am still evolving.

The Origin of the Species was commissioned by Monstrous Regiment. I had the luxury of a three-week exploratory workshop with the director, Nona Shepphard, and the two actors, Mary McCusker and Gillian Hanna. We wanted to do a play about EVERYTHING ... but we somehow ended up in the thick soup of assumptions and guesses, mainly written by men, which is the history of evolution. The assumptions and guesses of this play are about Woman. The soup is one I made. Human beings, as far as I know, are the only species who write plays. I may be as ill-informed as Robert Chambers's mayfly. We tadpoles may not have evolved as I have assumed

... we may yet become frogs. We may not, as Victoria in the play asserts, have crawled out of the water but, as Vilfredo Pareto says: 'Give me a fruitful error any time, full of seeds, bursting with its own corrections. You can keep your sterile truth for yourself.'

Two Marias, for Theatre Centre, was written for audiences of seventeen-year-old schoolgirls. I found the extraordinary story of Maria del Amor and Maria del Morte in a Sunday newspaper and it had hung in my brain until the time came to take it down and examine it. I was grieving over the sudden death of a friend, Philip Tyler, and this play, which returns the dead briefly to the living, helped me to work through my fury. The play was performed in school halls with the audience on four sides of a sunny Spanish courtyard. Although the girls enjoyed the piece, it was the teachers who were invariably moved to tears. I had been set to write a play for daughters and ended up writing one for mothers. It is a play for those scared of losing their loved ones to some unimaginable tragedy.

Her Aching Heart, for the Women's Theatre Group, started off as a worthy brief to write 'a two-hander exploring sexuality and gender'. Claire Grove (the director) and I felt somewhat mournful and sluggish about the project, until we discovered a mutual addiction to romantic fiction. We decided, courageously, to Come Out. Luckily I had spent my radiant teens alternately swotting for Latin, English and History 'A' levels and bunking off to read Georgette Heyer and Daphne du Maurier. Admirers of the British education system will discover in the text a cornucopia of romantic gush, at least five non-adjacent historical periods ... and five words of Latin.

Nothing Compares to You was commissioned by Gwenda
Hughes at Birmingham Rep. She wanted a 'small, girls'
love story . . . something light, something gothic'. Her
composure upon receiving a nine-hander which begins
with a woman sliced in two by a car, has creatures
called 'fylgia' which visit the Antarctic (stage direction
'*They ski down the mountainside*'), the Rain Forest, the
Galapagos Islands . . . and explores death, betrayal,
sexual jealousy, relationships, friendship and immortality
. . . was nothing short of heroic. One critic said 'Bryony
Lavery hasn't written the play she thinks she has . . .' Oh
mayfly . . . how very true.

Bryony Lavery
December 1997

Origin of the Species

Origin of the Species was first produced by Monstrous Regiment on 22 November 1984 at Birmingham Repertory Theatre Studio, with the following cast:

Molly	Gillian Hanna
Victoria	Mary MacCusker

Directed by Nona Shepphard
Designed by Jenny Carey
Administration Sandy Bailey

This production subsequently ran at the Drill Hall, London, from 20 March to 6 April 1985.

Part One

One: An old lady's room in Yorkshire

A very strange, very comfortable and unsettling room. In it – a comfortable, eccentric, healthy, intelligent, magnificent woman of indeterminate age. She is in the middle of a hearty snack of tea, toast and cake.

Molly Tea and toast.
Perhaps humanity's two most . . . resounding achievements.

She eats. She drinks.

The nice thing about being a batty old crone is that you don't have to go out on New Year's Eve.
You can say
'Party? No thank you dear I think I'll stay in, sit by the fire and eat too much.'
And while this fat belly down here gets on with the miracle of digestion . . . this splendid organ up here can tell you a story . . .
Are you sitting comfortably?
Then I'll begin.

Two: A year diary

Molly This is me diary of important dates . . .
The Story So Far . . . As *Woman's Weekly* would say . . .
January First . . . The Big Bang . . . that was how it all began, my lovelies . . . stars dying . . . exploding their elements . . . those ninety-one elements that make up you, me, this room . . . everything.
The beginning of time.

She turns the pages. We see how empty they are.

Nothing. Nothing. Nothing.

May the first. The Milky Way formed.

She turns the pages again.

Nothing. No . . .
September the ninth . . . our solar system appears
. . . Orion, the Big Bear, Little Bear, Cassiopeia
. . . there's a book with them all in up there
somewhere . . .
September fourteenth. The earth you and I live on is
formed.
We live on one of the younger stars.
I call it Baby Earth.
It is the setting of my story.
September twenty-fifth . . . micro-organisms, the first
signs of life on Baby Earth.
October the second, first rocks formed on Baby Earth.
Ninth . . . bacteria . . . and blue algae make their first
appearance.
November now.
Now, that's an interesting day . . . because the micro-
organisms invent sex!
November twelfth . . . the first plants start to grow
Look how far through the year we are.

She demonstrates with the book.

December . . . and nothing so far but stars . . . earth,
plants . . . and micro-organisms indulging in sex.
Monday the first of December . . . a significant oxygen
atmosphere develops on earth.

Cold air from the window.

Sixteenth of December . . . the first worms appear . . .
and my diary begins to fill with life . . . seventeenth . . .
invertebrates flourishing . . . eighteenth . . . first oceanic
plankton, trilobites . . . nineteenth . . . a Friday . . . the
first fish!
Also . . . the first vertebrates . . . backbone at last!
Saturday the twentieth . . . plants begin to leave the

water and colonise land . . . the twenty-first . . . the first
insects crawl . . . animals colonise land . . . twenty-second
. . . first amphibians . . . swimming . . . insects . . . flying.
Twenty-third. First trees.
First reptiles crawl on their bellies . . . their fat bellies.
December. Dinosaurs walk the earth.
Dear dinosaurs.
Twenty-sixth . . . first mammals suck milk.
Twenty-seventh . . . the first birds sing.

She makes a bird noise.

Twenty-eighth . . . the dinosaurs die.

Tears stand in her eyes.

Twenty-ninth . . . primates.
By this point, you and I would recognise Baby Earth . . .
there are seas, rivers . . . lakes . . . many many plants
and trees . . . fish, reptiles, animals . . . and the year is
ending . . .
The thirty-first of December.
New Year's Eve.
A robust character makes an appearance in my diary
at the bottom of the last page.
A mammal.
It is covered with hair and walks on all four of its limbs.
About four minutes to midnight on the last night of the
year . . .
it raises itself on its back legs
and looks around.
It is a new species called hominids.
It is the Origin of You and Me.

Three: Mister Right

Molly   Now, I'm one of those people who are very
good at finding things.
My mother once lost her engagement ring on the beach.

The next day I went and picked it up!
She gave me sixpence!
If you lose a contact lens
you come to me.
Take me to the vicinity you dropped it I'll go straight to
it.
From the age of sixteen onwards, I was looking for a
man.
I knew what I wanted and if I went to the right spot
I'd pick him up straight away.
I knew exactly what I wanted ... someone older than
me ... a great discoverer ... a great inventor ... he
would be brave, resourceful, strong ... and very very
hairy!
He would be someone who could stand on his own two
feet!
And if I could get to the right spot I'd pick him up
straight away!

Four: A slice of layer cake

Molly   Now, I don't know if you're familiar at all with
Tanganyika ... but there's a place there called the
Olduvai Gorge ...

She decides to cut herself a slice of layer cake.

It's a place where a great *knife* of water ... in the form
of a seasonal river ... has carved out a huge slice in the
side of the mountain ... as a result, what we have at
Olduvai Gorge is something rather like this piece of
layer cake ...

She demonstrates this with her layer cake.

And if you imagine an ant standing down here on this
doily, looking up at this layer cake towering above him
... that is what it feels like to be a human being
looking up at Olduvai Gorge!

And looking at these layers . . . what you are gazing at
is millennium upon millennium stacked neatly one upon
the other like layers of chocolate and vanilla.
Olduvai Gorge is an enormous layer cake of Time!
And each layer is packed with fossils!
And the man I set my heart on is somewhere here.
Archaeology's simply the art of knowing where to look
and then looking and looking until you find it.
To find my man
I joined Louis and Mary Leakey, the famous husband-
and-wife archaeological team on their dig at Olduvai
Gorge.

Five: The dig

Molly Don't know why it's called a 'dig'.
Digging's the last thing you do on them.
It's mostly outdoor housework.
Constant cleaning.

She picks up her brush.

That . . . to brush away four million years of dust.
Now . . . on this dig there'd been an absolutely thrilling
find.
Mary Leakey had gone out on her own . . . Louis had a
touch of flu . . . and she'd spotted a few scraps of bone
in sand in a deep gully . . . and she and Bernard . . .
that's Bernard Ngeneo . . . a *superb* assistant . . . had
been working on it for weeks . . . collecting a scrap here,
a shard there . . . and each night they'd sit assembling
this three-dimensional jigsaw . . .
and it was a skull.

Skull on desk.

It had a relatively large brain capacity and relatively
small teeth . . . suggesting it to be the skull of a highly-
evolved hominid . . . and they'd dated it at about four

million years old!
It seemed likely that here was our earliest ancestor!
Bernard Ngeneo kept referring to it as 'Great
Granpappy' which made us all honk!
It was a very happy dig.
The camp was full of . . . contentment.
Except for me.
I was waking every night . . . clammy with sweat . . . my
hands rigid and hooked.
My spine tingling.
I kept saying to myself . . . 'You're not in a horror film,
Molly, go back to sleep!'
But the feeling would not go away.
These attacks went on for five nights . . . and I thought
I was maybe catching a touch of Louis' flu . . . then on
the sixth day, New Year's Day, my birthday, I woke
very early and I was completely at peace.

Six: The find

Molly I got up.
I dressed.
I went outside the tent and it was dawn.
No one else was awake.
The sky was light.
I knew exactly where to go.
I followed the stream.
I went straight to the place in the dust.

She goes to the place.

I knelt down.

She kneels down.

And started to work with my brush.

She starts to work with her brush.

And the first thing I found was the foot.

The foot appears.

And the foot seemed to be attached to a leg.

She uncovers the leg up to the thigh. She finds the hand.

This is the hand.
It seemed possible . . . that . . . the body was . . .
complete.

She brushes away the dust, revealing the body.

I uncovered the face.

She uncovers the face.

And looked on the face of my four-million-year-old
ancestor.

She looks.

And
I
kissed its
lips
and my four-million-year-old ancestor
opened its eyes

It opens its eyes.

and stood up.

It stands up.

And I realised that what I
had found was
a woman.

Seven: Victoria

Molly   And I smuggled her back here to Yorkshire.
And I called her Victoria
after my grandmother.

Victoria   Ngagi!

All hell breaks lose. **Victoria**, *who is covered in hair, her arms longer than is normal today, her stance very different, rages round* **Molly**'s *room, looking for something familiar. She challenges and threatens* **Molly**. **Molly** *pours a saucer of milk and cuts up an apple . . . puts it on the floor.*

Molly   Shorter than me,
her pelvis narrower
the same species . . .
Less of a guzzleguts . . .
but the same species . . .

Victoria *goes under the table, where she feels safe. She starts to eat the apple and milk. She falls asleep.*

Less of a chatterbox . . .
but the same species . . .
Four million years ago,
in this head here,
there developed an organ,
whose job was merely to collect information about the
gathering of food
and below it this jaw
developed merely to produce a limited range of
articulated sound.
In this ball of bone here
is the origin of the human intellect . . .

Victoria *watches her as she gives her some more apple and milk.*

Apple . . . app-le.
Milk. Milk.
Apple. Milk.

Victoria *watchs her. She is calm.* **Molly** *gets a book, puts on some music.* **Victoria** *starts to connect. Finally . . .*

Victoria   Abb . . . al.

Molly *stops music.*

Victoria   Abb . . . al.

Molly   Yes . . . apple and milk.

Victoria   Abb-al an dmilg.

Molly   Yes.

Victoria   Ess!

Molly   Yyyy . . . es.

Victoria *bares her teeth in a yyy . . . but does not say yes.*

Molly   Listen to what Alfred Russell Wallace has to
say about brains like yours, Victoria:
'. . . seems as if the organ had been prepared in
anticipation of the future progress in man, since it
contains latent capacities which are useless to him in his
earlier condition.'
Man . . . him . . . his.

Victoria   Milg!

Molly *fetches milk.*

Molly   Milk . . . 'Natural selection could only have
endowed savage man with a brain a few degrees
superior to that of an ape, whereas he actually possesses
one very little inferior to that of a philosopher.'
He.

Victoria   Milg.

Molly   Yes! Milk!

Victoria   Ess! Milg!!!

Molly   Close your mouth when you're eating.

Victoria   Eee . . . ting!

Molly   My little apple-sauce factory.
You can write *Rigoletto*.
You can write *Middlemarch*.
You can watch your apple fall from its tree and

understand the law of gravity.
You can paint the ceiling of the Sistine Chapel.
You will produce great art.
You will produce great music.
You will invent you will discover you will make you will
do . . .
We call Africa
the Cradle of Mankind.
It is women in need who snatch babies from cradles.
I snatched my baby and set about looking after her.

Eight: Bringing up Baby

Molly *fetches clothing for* **Victoria**.

Molly   Come along Victoria, time to put your fig
leaves on.

She goes for clothes. **Victoria** *follows her.*

Homo erectus almost certainly invented clothing for
warmth,
not modesty
the warmth they needed as they moved to colder climes
in the search for food.
Victoria, you're in Yorkshire now lass, it's parky and I'm
going to have to tog you up.

She allows **Victoria** *to feel the cardigan.*

Yes, it's lovely and soft . . .

She starts to put **Victoria**'s *arm in the sleeve.* **Victoria** *pulls
it out.* **Victoria** *bares her teeth.*

Molly   Look, it won't hurt you . . .

She tries a bit of force. It doesn't work. **Molly** *takes off her
cardigan . . .*

Look, it's just like mine; you see, I'm putting it on and
I'm all right, I'm not hurt . . . I'm nice and warm . . .

see ... (**Victoria** *takes* **Molly**'s *cardigan off, which is warm.*)
... No, that's mine ... this one won't go with my frock
... oh never mind, do you want to wear that one then?

Victoria *wanders away with the cardigan.*

Molly   Right young lady!

Molly *takes a skirt ... using it as a sort of noose to trap*
Victoria, *which she succeeds in doing, being four million years*
younger.

Molly   Some girls ... would give their eye teeth for
... this ... argh ... nice skirt ...

Victoria   Gnee ... errh ... gneeh ... gneeh ...

Molly   You bastard ... you will ... this bloody skirt
... if it's the last thing I ... bloody do ...

Victoria   Gneeh ... urgh ... milg! ...

Molly   And now ... the socks ...

She has **Victoria** *on the ground and is sitting on her.*

I've got a few million years' start on you ... young lady
... the welfare state ... it's not bloody milg it's bloody
socks ...

Victoria   Gnee ... urgh ... ngagi ...

Molly   And now ... the cardigan ...
don't you bare those teeth at me young lady ... now
I'm just getting your other arm in ...
This is Yorkshire, miss, and we wear cardigans!

Finally she has her in skirt, socks and cardigan.

Now, who's a pretty girl?

Victoria *bites her.*

Molly   If ever ... a species deserved to ... die off ...
Victoria ...

Nine: The lesson

Molly   Once I had clothed her I was certain of two facts:
(a) she was protected against the vicissitudes of the bitter Yorkshire winter and
(b) if she escaped from my charge she would pass for one of my Yorkshire neighbours . . .
I then set about filling in the four-million-year gap between us.

Molly *moves around the room naming things.*

Apple.

Victoria   Abbal.

Molly   Banana.

Victoria   Bu-nan-a.

Molly   Bowl.

Victoria   Bowwll.

Molly   Chair.

Victoria   Tchair.

Molly   Book.

Victoria   Buk.

Victoria *picks up* **Molly***'s knitting.*

Molly   That's knitting.

Victoria   Nitt-tingg.

Molly   Yes . . . give it to me, you might hurt yourself . . . (*She pulls at the needles, they come off the wool.*) . . . be caref . . . oh dear . . . it's *wool* . . . and *needles* now! Never mind . . . clock . . .

Victoria   Clock . . . buk buk buk buk buk buk buk

Molly   She learned enormously quickly!

Molly *uses herself as a visual aid.*

Victoria   Hedd.
Syolders.
Byeasts.

She is starting to move each in turn.

Ahms.
Hahnds.

Molly *starts to hum 'The Charleston', and move in time to it.*

Victoria   Bost-ear-ia!
Phuts!

Molly   Although enormously older than me . . .
I treated her like a kiddie.

She starts showing **Victoria** *pictures.*

Victoria   Mahn.
Wuhman.
Lage.
Tee.
Busch.
Moon.
Sea.
Fol-cano.
C-y-ocodile.
Anch-e-lope.

Molly   Spoken language is incomparable as a vehicle
for the development and transmission of culture . . .

She shows the antelope again.

Victoria   Anmal.

Molly   No.

She shows her the crocodile.

Victoria   Anmal.

Molly   No.

She shows her the fish.

Victoria Anmal.

Molly (*smacks her hand*) Victoria . . . you *know* their names!

Victoria (*shown the three cards again*) Fis.
Cy-ocodile.
An-ch-e-lope.

Molly What's the matter, Down-In-The-Mouth?
Are you hungry?
Do you want another abb-al? Drink of milg?

Victoria Fis. Anmal.
Cyocodileanmal.
Anchelope anmal.

Molly *suddenly realises she is putting ideas together.*
She checks the fact. She takes pictures of a man, a woman etc.

Molly Man.

Victoria Anmal.

Molly Woman.

Victoria Anmal.

Molly Lake.

Victoria *looks blank.*
Molly *holds both picture of lake and woman.*

Victoria Woman. Anmal. Lage . . .

Molly Water.

Victoria War-du.

Molly Yes, water.

Victoria Ess! War-du.
War-du . . . milg.

Molly Yes! Water and milk! Animal animal animal

animal animal fish crocodile antelope man woman lake
water milk!

Molly's *voice chirrups with excitement.* **Victoria**, *a copying
animal, mimics the chirrups.*

Victoria   Ess! Ik! Mamahlmahmal mahmalmahmal! Fis!

Molly   And the days flew.
I don't know which is the greater joy . . .
the passing on of knowledge
or the receiving of knowledge . . .

*She gets a handful of different coloured buttons out of her button
box.*

These are buttons, Victoria.

Victoria   Bu-ddons.

Molly   Look, you've got some on your cardigan
and I've got some on mine.

She shows **Victoria** *how to button up her cardigan by buttoning
up her own.* **Victoria** *tries without success to do up a button.*

Molly   Now look . . . (*She lays out the buttons.*)
White. Yellow. Blue. Green. Black. Red. Brown.

Victoria *looks at the buttons.*

White button. Yellow button. Blue button. Green button.
Black button. Red button. Brown button.

Victoria *still looks at the buttons.*

Molly   OK, how do we do this? . . . Green button . . .
(*She takes it, puts it on an apple.*) . . . green apple.

Victoria *picks up the red button. She puts it on the apple.*

Victoria   Green abbal.

Molly   No. Green button. Green apple.
Red button. Red . . . book. (*She puts the red button on the*

red book.)
Green button. Green apple.
Red button. Red book.

Victoria *picks up the yellow button.*

Victoria   Buddon.

Molly   Yellow button.

Victoria   Yyyy-ellow buddon.

Molly   Yes . . . (*She gives* **Victoria** *a heavy clue by looking fixedly at the banana, then picking it up carelessly.*) . . . yellow button . . . yellow . . .

Victoria   Bu-nana!!!

Molly   Yes! Yellow banana!

Victoria   Ess! Yellow banana . . . yyyellow buddon!

Molly   Good girl!

Victoria *picks up a button at a time.*

Molly   Blue . . .

Victoria *starts looking for something blue.*

Victoria   Bloo buddon . . .

Molly   My dear dear Victoria . . .

Victoria   Bloo buk.

Molly   Yes . . . it's all in there, isn't it? All those colours . . . (**Victoria** *picks up another button.*) Brown.

Victoria   Brrowwn buddon.

The search continues.

Molly   There's places in that brain of yours for every single colour and thing and animal and plant isn't there?

Victoria   Browwwn . . . boddel.

Victoria *picks up a white button.*

Molly   White.

Victoria   Whidte buddon . . . whidte . . . sugger.

Molly   Good girl.

She puts the sugar lump in **Victoria**'s *mouth.*

Victoria   Anku.

Molly   You're welcome.

Victoria *gets another white button.*

Victoria   Whidte buddon. Whidte sugger.

She opens her mouth.

Molly   Have some tea instead. Brown tea.

Ten: Heat

Molly   It's better for your teeth.

Victoria *gnashes her teeth to show she understands.*

Molly   Yes teeth . . . white teeth . . . look at that,
dental decay . . . oh never mind, you won't need to
know that unless you have too much white sugar . . .

Victoria   Sugger!

She puts out her tongue for some.
Molly *pours tea.*

Victoria   Tung.
Sugger. Pyeeze.

She gazes at **Molly** *beseechingly.*

Molly   Tea.

She has the cup, **Victoria** *the saucer.*

Victoria   Whidte sugger pyeeze.

Molly   Oh for goodness' sake!

Molly *puts sugar in the saucer.*

Victoria   Anku.

Molly   Ugh. Freezing.
Should have kept it warm.

Victoria *is dipping her finger in the tea and licking it.*

Victoria   Ugh. Fyeezing.

Molly   Lady Muck. Wants fresh tea now.

Victoria *carries her saucer towards the fire.*

Molly   Aha-a-a Victoria, fire! Hot!

Victoria *backs off from the fire.*

Molly   Fire! You'll burn yourself.

Victoria *looks at the saucer, then at the fire.*

Victoria   Fi.

She shows **Molly** *how she is warming her saucer.*

Victoria   Fi.

Molly   Do you remember fire?

Victoria   Rrredd fi. Ess.

Molly   You used fire?

Victoria *(warming her saucer)*   Ess.
Wuhman.
Fi. Fictoryia. Fi.

Molly   Victoria used fire. Where did you get it from?
How did you make it?

Victoria   Fi. *(She stretches out her hand to it.)*

Molly   Yes!

She points to fire.

She points to **Victoria**.

You . . . fire . . . where?
Victoria . . . Molly . . . fire . . . Electricity Showrooms!

She mimes getting fire from outside.

Victoria . . . fire . . . (*She opens her arms, looks enquiring.*)
Where?

Victoria *looks. She goes to the pictures, comes back with two.
She shows one to* **Molly**.

Molly   Volcano.

Victoria   Ess. Redd.

She shows her the other picture.

Molly   Woman.

Victoria   Ess. Wuhman volcano fi.

Molly   Now just a minute.

She goes to the pictures, selects one.

Victoria   Mahn.

Molly   Yes. (*She substitutes the man for the woman.*)
Man volcano fire.

Victoria (*changes the pictures again*)   Wuhman volcano fi.

Molly   You got the fire from the red-hot lava of the
volcano.

Victoria   Fi. Vol-cano. Ess.

Molly   You did. Woman.

Victoria   Ess.

Molly   Woman. Not man? (*She is showing* **Victoria** *the
two pictures.*)

Victoria (*puts woman picture by volcano picture*)   Wuhman
volcano fi.

Molly   Woman. The great discoverer.
Discovered fire.

Victoria   Wuhman ... fi ... fis ... anmal ... (*She holds her saucer of tea over the fire.*)

Molly   No book, no paper, no learned tome I had ever dug through during my dusty days as a student of archaeology had made mention of this.
They said ... 'Man discovered fire.'
Man.
Where was he in all this?
Woman ... fire ...
Man ... ? (*She shows the picture.*)

Victoria   Mahn ... anmal ... leg ...

Molly   Was chasing animals ... hunting ...

Victoria   Wuhman ... busch ... (*Agitated.*) ... hahnd ...

Molly   She gathered plants ...

Victoria   Mahn ... wuhman ... sugger ...

Molly   And man and woman ate them. Animals and plants. Which he hunted and she gathered.

Victoria   Card-e-gan ... skyirt.

Molly   Clothes.

Victoria   Anmal ... anche-lope ...

Molly   She made from fur ...

Victoria   (*picks up the cake knife*)   Tone ...

Molly   Stone ... she took a stone ... a sharp stone ...

Victoria   Tone ... anmal ... card-e-gan ...

Molly   And with a sharp-edged stone tool, she scraped the skins of animals to make clothes.
She discovered how to use fire.

She learned how to use sharp stones as tools.
She. The great discoverer.
She. The great inventor.

Eleven: A defence

Molly   You'll be asking why I kept her. You'll be
wondering why I didn't hand her over.
Why did I smuggle her back here and keep her for
myself?
I want to read you something.
It's by a leading French scientist, called Gustave Le Bon.
He was one of the founders of social psychology. Listen
to what he had to say in 1879:
'In the most intelligent races, as among Parisians, there
are a large number of women whose brains are closer in
size to those of gorillas than to the most developed male
brains. This inferiority is so obvious that no one can
contest it for a moment; only its degree is worth
discussion. All psychologists who have studied the
intelligence of women, as well as poets and novelists,
recognise today that they represent the most inferior
forms of human evolution and they are closer to
children and savages than to an adult, civilised man.
They excel in fickleness, inconstancy, absence of thought
and logic, and incapacity to reason.
Without doubt there exist some distinguished women,
very superior to the average man, but they are as
exceptional as the birth of any monstrosity, as, for
example, a gorilla with two heads; consequently, we may
neglect them entirely.'
The most learned men of my time thought her an
object of little value.
If she'd been a pot of gold I'd have handed her in.
But . . . she was a gorilla with two heads.
She was just an old woman. And so was I.

It was a crime of passion, my dears.
I wanted her.

Twelve: Mothers and babies

Molly   Now my little inventor, discoverer, clothes-maker, plant-gatherer . . . why didn't you go hunting?

Victoria   Baby.

Her eyes spill with tears.

Molly   Oh . . . tell me about this baby, Victoria.

Victoria (*her eyes flood with tears*)   Baby.

Molly   Yes. Your baby?

Victoria *pats her chest.*

Molly   Aw . . .

Victoria   Baby wuhman.

Molly   It was a little girl . . . look at these tears . . . dear dear me . . . do you know, baby sea otters cry, Victoria . . . G. W. Steller, who studied sea otters said, 'I have sometimes deprived females of their young on purpose, and they would weep over their affliction, just like human beings.' . . . Aren't men *peculiar*, Victoria? Don't cry my little sea otter . . . my little apple-sauce maker . . .
What happened to your little girl?

Victoria   Anmal . . .

Molly   What kind of anmal?

Victoria   Cyo-codile . . .

Molly   Oh dear.
It's no comfort but actually crocodiles make very good mothers . . .
They lay their eggs in mounds of earth which they push together with their snouts and then the mothers stay by

the mounds for up to . . . but I expect you know that
. . . oh dear oh dear oh dear how can we stop these
tears?
Right!

She gets up, fetches a bottle of brandy.

Brandy.
Good for shock . . .
There's a country where people get buried in snow
Victoria . . .
and a great big dog anmal comes along with a barrel of
this round its neck . . . and it sniffs and searches until it
finds the person who's been buried and gives her a slug
of this and she perks up a treat . . .
grr . . . uff . . . rrr . . . owf . . . (*She imitates a St Bernard.*)
. . . ruffruffruffruff . . . ooohhooh!

Victoria *watches her. A slight smile.*

Molly   Drink your brandy, avalanche kid!

Molly *tosses her brandy down in one.* **Victoria** *watches, then
tosses her brandy down in one. Once it has gone down she opens
her mouth in a wide gag with her tongue out.*

Molly   Some milg now?

Victoria   Ess.

Thirteen: 'Auld Lang Syne'

Molly   You can have it in a cup now you're
sophisticated enough to drink brandy!

She pours her a cup of milk. **Victoria** *dips her finger in it.*

Molly   No, drink it . . . (*She sees that* **Victoria** *is drawing
on a piece of paper with her finger.*) Oh you're drawing . . .
(*She gets her a pencil.*) . . . red pencil, white paper. (*She
shows her how to do it.*) . . . See?

Victoria   Anku.

Molly   You're welcome.
A perfect evening. Art . . . (*She puts some music on.*) . . .
Music . . . (*She chooses a Mickey Spillane book.*) . . . Literature
. . . Aren't we a couple of ladies, Victoria?

She reads.
Victoria *brings over her drawing.*

Molly   Oh, let's see what you've drawn.

Victoria   Mahn.

Molly   A man, lying down. Yes . . .

Victoria   Ess.

Molly   This man standing next to him . . . he's holding
a stone . . .

Victoria   Tone.

She taps **Molly** *on the head.*

Molly   The man with the stone is hitting the lying-
down man over the head.

Victoria   Ess.

Molly   What's that?

Victoria   Hedd.

Molly   It's the lying-down man's head?

Victoria   Ess.

Molly   What's that woman doing sitting by his head?

Victoria   Tone.

Molly   She's got a sharp stone, too?

Victoria   Ess.

Molly   What's she doing with the sharp stone?

Victoria   Ee-ting.

Molly   She's eating the lying-down man's brains.

Victoria   Ess.

Molly   Is this woman eating the lying-down man's brains . . . you?

Victoria   Ess.

Silence.

Molly   You eat . . . people?

Victoria   Nod mudge.

Molly   Oh goodness.

Victoria   Budd nod mudge.
One day
old wuhman . . . (*She touches her breast.*) . . .

Molly   Your mother?

Victoria   Mo-ther . . . ess . . . ill . . . stob gathering berries . . . roodts . . . stob may-king food. Stob . . . (*She touches* **Molly**'*s palm with her hand.*) . . . warm . . . stob . . . (*She breathes into* **Molly**'*s hand.*)

Molly   She died.

Victoria   Died.
Sahd.
I ahnd wuhmans tage mo-ther vrom camp.
Pud hurr away.
I and wuhmans tage sjarp tools
and holding hedd, cudd into brain and eet hurr.
Cud body and with fi burned itt.
I and wuhmans eet . . . leggs ahms and cheegs
miggsed bones ashes wid dyink and dyinked it.

Pause.

Molly   Why?

Victoria   I and mo-ther same.
She . . . (*She breathes into* **Molly**'*s palm.*) . . . in me.

Vict-oryia.
Molly die.
I eet Molly.

She gives **Molly** *a loving smile.*

Idden thadd why Molly dig Victoryia upp?

Lights fade.

Part Two

Fourteen: A song

Victoria *is wearing a beautiful kimono. She is impeccably if outrageously attired.* **Molly** *is wearing an old lady's nightie and a comfortable dressing-gown. Both have paper hats on.*

Molly   Ready?

Victoria   Ready.

Molly *goes and sits at the harmonium. They perform the following song, not magnificently but with great verve: 'On Ilkley Moor Bah T'At'.*

Victoria   Where hasta bin sin I saw thee?

Molly   On Ilkley Moor bah t'at.

Victoria   Where hasta bin sin I saw thee?

Both   Where hasta bin sin I saw thee?

Molly   On Ilkley Moor bah t'at.

Victoria   Bah t'at.

Molly   On Ilkley Moor bah t'at.

Victoria   Bah t'at.

Both   On Ilkley Moor bah t'at.

Victoria   Tha's gonna cotch thee death of cold.

Molly   Achoo.

Victoria   Then we shall atta bury thee.

Molly   Rest in peace.

Victoria   Then worms'll come and eat thee up.

Molly   Chomp chomp.

Victoria   Then ducks'll come and eat up worms.

Molly   Quack quack quack.

Victoria   Then we shall come and eat up ducks.

Molly   Yum yum.

Victoria   Then we shall all have eaten thee.

Molly   What a treat.

Both
On Ilkley Moor bah t'at.
On Ilkley Moor bah t'at.
On Ilkley Moor baaaah t'at.

Victoria   Plaie id again Molly! Plaie id again!

Molly   Of all the piano bars in all the towns in all the world . . . and she walks into my piano bar!

Victoria   Plaie id again Molly . . . p-leeze!

Molly (*plays and sings*)
You must remember this
A kiss is still a kiss
A sigh is still a sigh
The fundamental things apply
As time goes by . . .

Victoria   I doand know this one Molly . . .

Molly   The name's Sam, shweetheart . . . (*Sings:*)
It's shtill the same old shtory
A fight for love and glory
A case of do or die
The fundamental things apply
As time goes by . . .

Victoria   Id's nodd a piano.
Id's a hah-moan-i-yum.

Molly   Shweetheart . . . if Sham says it's a piano, it's a piano.

Victoria   Whad are you plaieing at?

Molly   It's called 'pretend'.

Victoria Eggsplain p-leeze.

Molly Yes, your majesty. This is a harmonium.

Victoria Yez.

Molly But if I say . . . Thish is my piano . . . I'm pretending.

Victoria Id's a hah-moan-i-yum Molly!

Molly I *know* it's a harmonium Victoria!
But I am playing a game . . . with myself.
I am really Molly Starkey, sitting in my room in Yorkshire, playing my harmonium to my friend Victoria . . . but I *pretend* I am called Sam and I am sitting in a sleazy bar in Casablanca playing a piano to Ingrid Bergman.

Victoria Have you been dringing the brandy?

Molly No, Ingrid.

Victoria You're nodd maging sense!

Molly I am using my imagination.

Victoria Where?

Molly Inside my head.

Victoria I want some inside my hedd!

Molly All right.

She lays her hands on **Victoria***'s head like a magician.*

Abracadabera Molly kazoo
Put some of that imagination
In Victoria's head too!

Victoria Iz id in?

Molly Yes, it's in!
OK . . . when I point to something . . . you can call it by a different name because you've got the imagination in your head now . . . OK?

Victoria   Okayy!

Molly (*points to her hand*)   Oh Victoria . . .
look at your . . .

Victoria   Phut!

Molly   The imagination is in there!
Victoria . . . look at my . . . (*She points to her eye.*)

Victoria   Mooowth!!!

Molly   Yes!

Victoria   Oh Molly look at your . . . (*She touches* **Molly**'s
breasts.) bosterior!

Molly   Oh yes I thought we'd have to have that one . . .

Victoria *runs round to her posterior.*

Victoria   Oh Molly, look at your breasts!

Molly   Yes, yes . . .

Victoria (*pointing at a chair*)   Oh Molly, look at the
laffatory . . . Oh Molly, look at the (*She points to food.*) . . .
eggscrement!

Molly   All right, that's enough rude ones . . .

Victoria (*goes to the grandfather clock . . . but says*)   Hello
Molly!

She points to **Molly**, *but talks to the clock.*

Look Molly . . . look at the clock . . . Molly, why do you
have hands on your face?

Molly (*to the chair*)   Victoria . . . would you like to pull a
cracker with me? . . . I know how you like pulling crackers
. . . (*To* **Victoria**:) . . . Excuse me chair . . . (*To the clock:*)
Molly . . . I'm just going to pull a cracker with Victoria over
there . . .

Victoria (*goes for a cracker . . . to the clock*)   Molly, would you
like to pull a cracker with me . . . eggscuse me clock. (*This to*

Molly. *She stands before the clock with the cracker.* **Molly** *stands before the chair.*)

Molly   Now I think you understand that, don't you Victoria?

Victoria   Yes Molly.
Pull a banana?

They pull two crackers.

Fifteen: Some strange rituals

Molly   Oh, I've got a little chain in mine!
What have you got, Victoria?

Victoria   A liddle mouse!

Molly   Lovely . . . where's my motto? (*Reading:*) 'What is the definition of an archaeologist?'

Victoria   I don't know . . . whad iz the definition of and archaeologist?

Molly (*reads*)   'A man whose career is in ruins.'

She screws up the paper and throws it away.

Victoria (*reads*)   'Whad is worse than raining cats and dogs?'

Molly   I don't know, what is worse than raining cats and dogs?

Victoria   'Hailing taxis.' (*Looks.*) I doand gedd it.

Molly   Well . . . never mind . . .

Victoria   Whad happens at twelve o'clock?

Molly   The old year ends.
The new year . . .
You become a year older.
I become a year older.

We have a glass of sherry . . .
Not yet . . .
And if I die of the excitement of it all . . . you cut off my biceps, triceps, my *vastus extenus, rectus femoris* and my cheegs . . . pop them into a Harvey's Bristol Cream and . . . (*She demonstrates tossing off a large sherry.*)

Victoria   And if I die of the eggsitement of it all . . . you pud me in a boggs like a big cigar and szmoke me!

She takes a cigar out of a box on the desk.

With . . . Firre!
I dizcovered!
Or pud me in a boggs and pud me in a deep hole you haff digged witth a ss . . . h . . . arp tool!
I invended!

There is a frosty silence.

Molly   What's wrong with you, crab apple?

Victoria   Nuthing.

Molly   There's a frosty silence.

Silence.

Why is there a frosty silence?

Victoria   Use your imagination.

She selects a chocolate and eats it.

Molly   Please may I have a chocolate?

Victoria   No.
These choglates are mine.

Molly   Capitalist.

Victoria   Whad's that?

Molly   An insult.
Please.

Victoria   Use your imagination.

Molly   Oh . . . Bugger!

Victoria   Bugger . . . bugger bugger bugger bugger . . .

Molly   All right. I'm sorry.
I don't know what I did
but I'm sorry.

Victoria   Doand mage fun of me.

Molly   OK.

Victoria   I am learning as vast as I can.

Molly   OK.
Sorry.
Now can I have a bloody chocolate?

Victoria   Yes

She selects a chocolate for **Molly**.

Molly   I don't like Chartreuse Creams.

Victoria   I don't like Chartreuse Creams either.
Mage fun . . . mage a cage . . . mage a fire . . . mage a
miztage . . .

Molly   Make a pig of yourself with all those
chocolates . . .

Victoria   How do you mage fun, Molly?

Molly   Oh not now Victoria . . . it's nearly . . .

Victoria   Now! I wand to know now!

Molly   Never a moment's rest is there? (*She picks up a
banana.*) You see this cracker?

Victoria   Heehee yyyess!

Victoria *laughs.*

Molly (*puts it down*)   That's how you make fun. (*She picks up
book to start reading.*)

Victoria   That's using immagginashion!

Molly   That's right . . . using imagination to make fun . . . flour and fat to make cake . . . wood and coal to make fire . . .

Victoria   It mages me laugh!

Molly   That's what fun's all about. (*She really is more interested in her book.*)

Victoria   I want to mage fun!

Molly   Yes . . . you go ahead . . . make fun . . . (*She reads.*)

Victoria *sits at the desk.*

Victoria (*to the skull*)   Hello Molly! . . . do you wand a choglate? It will mage you fat! . . . you cand have a choglate Molly, no! . . . did you eat my choglate Molly? . . . you badd woman! (*She picks up one of her crayons.*) . . . I'll hurt your eye!

She is working this out quietly to herself. **Molly** *is reading.*
Victoria *picks up the skull, chocolate and pencil, and goes over to* **Molly**.

Victoria   I'm going to mage fun!

Molly   Oh good.

Victoria (*brings out the skull*)   Hello Molly!
Whad? You wand a choglate? No, you cand have one!

Molly *is amused. The skull eats the chocolate.*

Victoria   Didd you eatt the choglate? Molly, didd you eat the choglate? (*To* **Molly**:) Didd Molly eat the choglate?

Molly   Yes she did, Victoria, I saw her, she took it and she swallowed it!

Victoria   You badd girll! I'll stigg this knife (*She produces a pencil.*) in your mowthh! (*She sticks the pencil in the skull's eye.*)

Molly   No. No. That's not making fun. (*She takes the pencil and skull.*) That's a pencil. We don't use pencils as weapons, Victoria. Not in this house. We don't hurt people, not even when we're making fun. (*She puts them back on the desk.*)

Victoria I was maging fun!

Molly Yes ... well ... sometimes making fun goes
wrong ...

Victoria Whad's a weapon?

Molly Never you mind. Do some drawing.

Victoria Whad's a weapon?

Molly I'm not going to tell you. Now shut up!
Let me read my bloody book in peace!

Victoria *is furious. She stands glowering. She goes to the bookcase,
gets out a dictionary, and laboriously finds 'weapon'.*

Victoria (*reads*) 'Weapon *n.* one an object or instrument
used in fighting two anything that serves to get the better of
an opponent his power of speech was his best weapon three
any part of an animal that is used to defend itself to attack
prey etc. such as claws or a sting OE wæpen weaponed *adj.*
weaponless *adj.*'
Id wont go in.
Id wont go in.
Id wont go in.

Molly All right, all right ...

Victoria Id all keeps going away ...

Molly Yes ...

Victoria I think I understand and then you tell me
something else and it all goes away!

Molly All in good time!

Victoria Id wont go in wont go in id wont go in!!!

Molly It will.
Shall we have some music on?

Pause.

Victoria Yess!

Music.

Sixteen: Music

Molly   If music be the food of love . . .

She presses a button.

. . . play on . . .

Music plays.

Let other folks listen to Jimmy Shand and his band.
My friend Victoria and I
will see the New Year in
with Miss Jacqueline du Pré . . .

They listen.

Victoria   Id was New Year when you digged me up.

Molly   Yes.

Victoria   Id was your birthday.

Molly   Yes.
What a New Year!
What a birthday.

Victoria   Yess!

Molly   New Year in Tanganyika!
Very different from Yorkshire.
Much better!

Victoria   Much bedder!

Molly   And look what I found!
It's not every New Year you find a Victoria.
Statistically . . . it's . . . rare.

Victoria   Molly . . .

Molly   Yes.

Victoria Why did you come to get me?

Molly Why did I come to get you? Do you really want to
know?

Victoria Yess!

Molly I didn't come to get you.

Victoria You didd.

Molly No. I came to get a man.

She turns the music off.

I was born in a time when it was all man . . . him . . . his . . .
all my books were about man . . . him . . . his . . . all my
music . . .
man him his . . . all that was important . . .
man him his . . . so what I was looking for was man . . . him
. . . my earliest ancestor on my father . . . him . . . his . . .
side.
So you can imagine my surprise on finding . . . you.

Victoria You didden want me.

Molly I didn't know you were there to want.

Victoria I was . . . seggond besd.

Molly Yes.
But the second I saw you
I stopped looking for a man
and I looked
at you.

Seventeen: The mayfly and the frog

Victoria Why?
Why didd you loog at me?

Molly I wanted to study you.

Victoria Why?

Molly   To see if you were like me.

Victoria   Why?

Molly   I wanted to know where I came from.

Victoria   Why?

Molly   To see if we were the same.
To see if I looked like my ancestor . . . to see . . .

Victoria   Of course you would.

Molly   There was no of course about it. You know the pond.

Victoria   Yess.

Molly   In April . . . what was hovering over the surface of
the pond in April?

Victoria   Flies.

Molly   Yes.
And what was . . . in the pond?

Victoria   Fissh.

Molly   And on that April day . . . for a time . . .
something else . . .

Victoria   Tadpoles!

Molly   Tadpoles! OK . . . now . . . I am a fly hovering
over the pond watching the tadpoles swimming about.

Victoria   Yess!

Molly   And as a fly . . . I live for just that one day.

Victoria   Yes.

Molly   And that day I look and I see . . .

Victoria   The tadpoles swimming.

Molly   And then . . . I die.

Victoria   Yess.

Molly   What do the tadpoles do then?

Victoria (*thinks*)   They . . . changed into frogs.

Molly   Yes. They lost their gills . . . their tails disappeared
. . . their legs developed
. . . and they crawled out of the pond onto the land.
All that change . . . and I wasn't there to see it.
I really just wanted to see how alike we were . . . my
ancestor and me.

Eighteen: The aquatic ape

They look at one another.

Victoria   Hello fryogg.

Molly   Hello . . . frog.

Victoria   For mudge of the time I lived in the water.

They stare at one another.

Tadpole.
Yess.
I swam.
I dived.
I held my breath and dived.
In the water I called like . . . the dolphin.
To see in the water . . .
I cried like the sea otter.
My baby was heavy like the seal.
She swam in the water with me hanging to the thigg hair of
my head.
I lived in the water like the dolphin, the seal, the sea otter
. . . nodd the monkey.
I swam. I dived.
I dived deep.
It got darker.
The water thicker.
Then I felt something

touching my foot
my leg
my hand
my face
my lips
and I opened my eyes
and saw
my four-million-year-old descendant
standing up on the ground
and it was then I realised that what had
found me was
a woman
And she smuggled me back here to
Yorkshire
and she called me
Victoria
after her grandmother.

Nineteen: Identical twins

Victoria   We are the same.
I can do everything you can do now, Molly.

She picks up the skull.

When you found me I was like this and now . . . (*She comes
and puts her hand on* **Molly**'s *head.*) . . . I'm like this . . .
Abracadabra Molly kazoo . . . full of imagination too . . .
This is all in here now.
This is just like this.
Identical twins.

Molly   If that's so, my little two-headed gorilla, that
brain'll be forming a few questions.

Twenty: Some questions

Victoria *thinks.*

Victoria   You alwayss knew I was the same.
You kept me here and helped me
to think
and to sspeag.
Why Molly?
What do you want me for?

Twenty-one: Some answers

Molly   I want you to take off my shoes.

Victoria *goes down on her knees and takes off* **Molly***'s slippers.
Underneath are bandages.*

Molly   Undo the bandages.

Victoria *undoes the bandages to reveal hideously deformed feet.*

Victoria   Why did they do that?

Molly   So I couldn't run away.

Victoria   Does it hurt?

Molly   Yes.
Open this.

She points to her dressing-gown. **Victoria** *pulls aside her dressing-
gown. Underneath is a whalebone corset.*

Victoria   What is this for?

Molly   So I can't breathe.
Do I look pretty?

Victoria   No.

Molly   Now these.

Victoria *takes off her gloves.* **Molly***'s hands are burned.*

Victoria   Is this to make you look pretty?

Molly   I used to heal with these hands.
So they burned them.

You can't see what they did to my brain.
It's inside.
This is why I kept you.
I didn't want you to come to any harm.

Victoria   Who did it to you?

Twenty-two: The clock story

Molly   Once upon a time
Baby Earth was born
and Baby Earth grew up and became in time
a mother of many children
of many different kinds and sorts and shapes and sizes
and some were plants and some were fish and some were
crocodiles and some were humans were men were boys
and one day one of the boys invented
a clock out of sharp stones
and fire
it's a clock it's a clock it's a clock
ticking into your ear
and the clock told the time
and every child of every kind and sort and shape and size
admired the clock what a powerful clock
and the boy became rightly proud of the fine big powerful
clock he had
and he strutted and preened and looked around holding his
fine big powerful clock
and suddenly
as if a mighty lens had fallen over his eye
he saw that everything
looked like a clock
look he said everything is really a clock . . . this fish is a
clock this crocodile
is a clock this man is a clock this woman is a clock this child
is a clock
I think my mother is a clock!
And he took a sharp tool and stuck it into his mother's

stomach
and the knife ran red with blood
oil he said
and twisted the knife
he heard screams
ticking he said
and pulled out the knife
full of guts
ah cogs and wheels he said
now I know how this thing works
and he started taking apart the clock that was his
mother . . .
to see what she was made of.

Victoria   What was the boy's name?

Molly   Oh, he had a string of fine names . . .
he was called
Plato Aristotle Copernicus Galileo Bacon Descartes Newton
and because he was so interested in clocks he began to take
apart other clocks man clocks woman clocks animal clocks
plant clocks so soon his home was littered and strewn with
pieces
of the different clocks
and the odd thing was
the more he took the clocks apart with his sharp instruments
the less they seemed to work
the less they ticked
the stiller the cogs and wheels were
the oil dried
things turned brown and rotted away
doesn't matter he said
they're just clocks
so he assembled a new set of clocks
he made digging clocks and burrowing clocks and whizzing
clocks and firing clocks and exploding clocks
and soon there was no clock he could not make
finally he made a clock which could make
everything vanish

this is my best clock he said
my vanishing clock
I must take this and show it to my mother
and he ran with his vanishing clock
hither and thither
but his mother had vanished
and he looked at his exploding clock
and saw that he had very little time left.

They look at the clock.

Victoria   Is there going to be a New Year?

Molly   I don't know.

Victoria   What happened to him?

Molly   He's outside.

Victoria   Now?

Molly   With his vanishing clock.

Victoria   Why didn't anyone stop him?

Molly   No one has found a way of stopping him.

Victoria   I'll stop him.

Twenty-three: The presents

Molly   In that case, you'd better have your presents.
Usual place Victoria.

Victoria *goes to where she was dug up. She uncovers a wrapped box. She brings it back and opens it. In it is a pair of sensible shoes and a warm coat.*

Molly   It's bitter out.
I don't want you catching cold.

Victoria *puts the coat and shoes on.*

Molly   Little surprise in the pocket

Victoria *puts her hand in the pocket and brings out a pair of gloves.*

Molly   You know what they say . . .
'Cold hands, warm heart'.
Only old ladies stay in on New Year's Eve . . . everybody
else goes out and enjoys themselves.

She adjusts **Victoria***'s coat.*

Off you go then . . .
Remember who you belong to.

Victoria *waits.*

Molly   Bye bye then love.

Victoria *exits.*

Twenty-four: Survival of the fittest

Molly   I wasn't going to give you it all.
But . . . you need to know.
Greater knowledge implies a greater chance of survival . . .
that's what evolution is all about . . .
and . . .
although extinction is the ultimate fate of all species . . .
and not just the lot of unfortunate and badly-designed
creatures . . .
extinction's no sign of failure.
Ninety-eight per cent of all species are now extinct.
I can live without the dinosaur.
I can live without the dodo . . . even though a pigeon the
size of a turkey would be something to see!
I can do without the Nubian wild ass, the panda, the
Caribbean monk seal, the blue whale . . . I could even . . .
when pushed . . . manage without the square-lipped
rhinoceros . . .
but the passing of you,
Victoria,
that would break my heart.

Twenty-five: The end of the year

Molly   Midnight.
End of the year.

We hear the clock strike.

Bong!
Bong!
Bong!
Bong!
Bong!
Bong!
Bong!
Bong!
Bong!
Bong!
Bong!
Bong!

There is a silence.

Where are you then?

Music is heard.

Happy New Year!
Happy Birthday!
Glass of Harvey's Bristol Cream?
Why nodd?

Two Marias

Two Marias was first performed by Theatre Centre Women's Company in October 1989 with the following cast:

Marguerita	Janet Jeffries
Maria	Tracey Anderson
Julia	Rosy Fordham
Maria del Morte	Angella Wellington

Directed by Libby Mason
Designed by Vonnie Roudette
Music by Jacky Tayler

A courtyard outside a Spanish house. There are benches, chairs, terracotta pots on three sides. On the fourth side, the house. The ground is dusty. There is fierce light and heat in some of the courtyard, deep cool shade elsewhere.

Marguerita, *a fifty-year-old woman, enters, carrying a bag. She looks towards the house.*

Marguerita   This house here is full of pain.
Feel it in my heart.
Oh ... the ache.
It answers mine.
Lay your hand upon the forehead of this house.
Flap your wings and cool the heat here.

She sits in the deep shade on one of the benches, takes a newspaper from her bag and fans herself with it.

Maria, *a young woman, enters at a rush from the house. She flings herself down on one of the benches.*

Maria (*absolute conviction*)   I *hate* my mother!!!

Marguerita (*to herself*)   Aye ... dear!

Maria   Hate her, hate her ... hate her bones and her face and her foul foul mouth!!!

*From the house we hear **Maria**'s mother's voice.*

Julia   Get back in this house!

*No response from **Maria**.*

I want to talk to you!

No response.

Now, if not sooner!

No response.

Maria!!!
Please!!! (*It is not a request.*)

Marguerita (*to herself*)   Maria!

Maria (*scornful*)   Please!!!

Julia   Maria!!!

Marguerita (*looking at the girl*)   Maria . . .

Julia enters from the house.

Julia   How *dare* you walk out when I am talking to you?

Maria   How *dare* you talk to me like that???

Julia   You ill-mannered little . . . bitch!!!

Maria   You rude old . . . cow!!!

Julia   You what????

She comes towards **Maria**.

Maria   Just try it, Mama!!! Just you try it!!!!

They go to opposite sides of the courtyard, radiating hatred.

Julia   You cannot do this!! You cannot!!
You are my daughter and you will bring shame on me!

Maria   I have done it! It has happened!
You're my mother! You should be pleased for me that I've . . .

Julia   Pleased!!! Pleased for you? I should kill myself and you!!!

Maria   I've done nothing wrong!

Julia   Nothing wrong? God help us!

Maria   I have fallen in *love* . . . that's all!

Julia   Love? Love? Shut up!

Maria   No!!!
In love . . . *love* . . . with a beautiful, wonderful, kind, intelligent person . . .

Julia   Person? She is a *girl*! You can't!

Maria Yes, she is a girl! I can!

Julia You're mad!

Maria I'm not!

Julia You're sick!

Maria It's not a disease . . .

Julia You need locking up!

Maria It's not a crime!

Julia I wish you'd never been born!!!

Absolute silence.

Maria Mama.

Julia *looks away. Neither can speak.*

Julia *sees* **Marguerita** *sitting in the shade.*

Marguerita Just a little rest . . . then I'm on my way. Hot as hell, heh?

Marguerita *folds her newspaper in a certain way, takes a glass or two from her bag. Pours two glasses of water from the paper. She takes one glass to* **Julia**.

Marguerita Daughters, eh?

Takes the other glass to **Maria**.

Mothers eh? Salud!

Julia Señora . . . I don't think . . . this is . . .

Marguerita Señora . . . I'm a stranger passing through . . . It's not important.

Maria Not important! My life!!

Julia Your life? What kind of life is that??? No husband, no children, no family . . . everyone despising you? You'll have no life!

Marguerita Not important, I should know . . .

Señorita . . . important for you of course . . . front page
stuff . . . headlines ten centimetres high!
(*She reads from the newspaper.*) 'Foreign News . . . The
English *Times* reports the death in Chelmsford of a
middle-class woman who had been kept secluded in a
barred and darkened house for fifty years by her
mother, who disapproved of her friendship with an army
officer.' Six lines . . . words . . . this high . . . for fifty
years of no sun, no freedom, no love . . . ttt . . . tttt . . .
salud!

Maria   It's done . . . you can't stop me.

Julia   I'll take you to the priest . . . I'll take you to the
doctor . . . what's your father going to . . .

Maria   You're driving me senseless!

Julia   And what do you think you're doing to me?
You're making me crazy!!!

Maria   You're suffocating me!

Julia   Maria . . . Please!!!

Maria   No!!!
I love her!

Julia   Shut up! Shhh!

Marguerita (*taking out a pair of scissors and folding up a
piece of newspaper, she starts snipping*)   Another small story.
'Tom Hansen, fifteen, has taken out the first ever
parental malpractice suit against his mother and father.
He is suing his parents for $350,000, claiming they
made his childhood a misery. Hansen says he was
treated so badly he will need psychiatric care for the rest
of his life.'

She unfolds the paper. There is a line of figures.

Tttt . . . tttt!

She tears off the end figure carefully.

Tom Hansen.

She gives the figure to **Maria**.

Julia I'd better make supper.

Maria I'm not hungry.

Marguerita I am.

Julia Señora . . . excuse me . . . I . . . it's not . . .

Marguerita Convenient? It is for me . . . I'm hungry
. . . for food . . . for company . . . for a little sit . . .

Maria She can have my supper. Make it for her.

Julia Maria . . .

Maria I don't want it! And you don't want me! Not
me like I am, like I really am . . . sitting down in your
respectable house, eating your respectable food, at your
respectable table . . .

Julia Shut up!

Marguerita This one doesn't want your food . . . you
don't want this one talking . . . I want food . . . talk . . .

Maria Give her what she wants, Mama. Food and
company for the mad woman.

Julia You be quiet!

Marguerita The mad woman.

Julia Señora . . . I'm sorry . . . it's not . . . at the
moment . . . it's not . . . the right time.

Marguerita Oh it is . . . it is the right time. Please. I
have brought something with me . . .

Julia What . . .

Marguerita I have brought my dead daughter.

There is complete silence.

Marguerita (*takes newspaper cuttings and photographs from her bag*) She exists only here. (*She shows them.*) She lives now only in my heart. (*She sits at her bench and waits.*)

From the bench and through the disarray of newspapers emerges her daughter, **Maria del Morte**.

Marguerita   Her name was Maria also. She died two years ago.

Julia   Señora . . . I . . . what happened?

Marguerita   This happened. Imagine it. It is a hot summer night. My daughter Maria decided to go for a swim. She said goodbye. Imagine too, that your daughter Maria also decided to go for a swim. She says goodbye. It is eight-thirty, 2 June 1987 and your Maria's car rounds the final curve that leads through the pine woods to the long beach at Punta Umbria. Suddenly, a car in the opposite lane swerves off the asphalt and throws up a shower of gravel which shatters the windscreen of the Renault behind. Blinded, the driver of the Renault veers into the oncoming lane and, at forty miles an hour, slams into the car carrying your daughter. She breaks her ankle frantically trying to brake . . . then crushes her chest on the steering wheel as the force of the crash heaves her, face first, through the windscreen.

Julia   God in heaven!

Maria del Morte   I was the driver of the Renault. (*She sits down beside* **Maria**.) I too was a young woman. I too was called Maria.

Maria   Mama . . . I'm scared.

Marguerita   Of course you are! You're alive!

Maria del Morte   Mother . . .

Marguerita   Yes . . . yes yes yes.

Maria del Morte   Suppose the two of us, the drivers,

were sitting side by side on a bench. I was tall and slender with light brown hair. She, like you, had a pug nose, slightly plumper ... with short chestnut hair ... and a brace on her teeth. Nobody could have mistaken us for each other. But that was what happened.

Marguerita   That Saturday, two years ago, the road was jammed ... with pilgrims going to the shrine at El Roscio ... it took the ambulance an hour to reach ... to get to the ... the accident ...

Maria del Morte   By the time it arrived ... the other girl was barely alive ... and I was dead. We were put in the ambulance side by side and driven to the Residencia Hospital at Huelva. On the floor of the ambulance, between us, were our handbags. In the handbags were our names. Mine ... Maria del Morte. Hers ... Maria del Amor. In the confusion and pain and blood ... the handbags were switched. So, simply ... I was pronounced alive. The other Maria was pronounced dead.

Marguerita   At the hospital ... the parents of Maria del Amor asked to see the body of their daughter ... the authorities advised them against it ... saying that the corpse was in too terrible a state ... and they did not want them to remember their daughter that way.

Maria del Morte   I was a dreadful sight! (*She smiles.*) So, while the new Maria del Morte lay ill in hospital I was buried, as Maria del Amor, in a strange cemetery, seventy miles from my home ... mourned by a family I had never met.

She gets up and lights candles. The smell of incense fills the courtyard.

Julia   What did her mother do?

Marguerita   What would you have done?

Julia   I would leave her room just as it was ... the

night she left for the beach . . . the clothes . . . all her stupid 'fashionable' clothes . . . all over the bed, the chairs . . . left it untidy . . .

Maria   It's not untidy.

Julia   It is. You are.

Marguerita   That is what she did.

Julia   And at night . . . I would light a candle and put it in the window, to guide her soul back through the darkness.

Maria   I have no soul. I don't believe . . .

Julia   You have. You do.

Marguerita   That is what she did.

Maria del Morte   And what of the mother of Maria del Morte?

Marguerita   I . . . my husband . . . Antonio, my son . . . go to the hospital. She has been transferred to Seville . . . she is very ill . . . very very ill . . . we go to Seville . . . (*She gets up and goes to* **Maria**.) She is in a coma. (*She sits down by* **Maria**.) Her eyes are closed. (*She closes* **Maria**'s *eyes*.) She is swathed in bandages. (*She touches her face.*) Her body is all broken. (*She touches her body.*) For eighteen days . . . she is in a coma. When the bandages are unwrapped her face is criss-crossed with stitch-marks, swollen and bruised. (*She looks at* **Maria**.)

Maria del Morte   My brother . . . Antonio . . . questioned later by a newspaper reporter . . . says 'Not for a minute, did we ever doubt it was my sister!!!'

Marguerita   We were only allowed to see her for two, three minutes a day!!

Maria del Morte   Me!!!!

Marguerita   I was all the time praying that you would live!!!!

Maria del Morte *turns away . . . she picks up the newspaper figures . . . reads.*

Maria del Morte   'Barbara Avery, seventeen, was convicted today of killing her thirty-nine-day-old daughter Tominka, in an incinerator because she wanted to go to her own birthday party and could not find a baby-sitter. When she could not find a sitter, she dropped the baby into the incinerator and went to the party.'
(*She tears off a cut-out person and holds it in the candle.*)
Tominka Avery. (*It smoulders.*)

Marguerita   Barbara Avery.

Maria del Morte *crumples another cut-out figure in her hand.*

Maria del Morte   When Maria del Amor woke from her coma, after eighteen days, she had lost all memory of who she was.

Julia   The poor child.

Maria   She remembered nothing at all?

Marguerita   She remembered how to eat . . . how to talk . . . she talked a little . . . she could understand . . . read newspapers . . .

Maria   She did not remember . . . who her mother was?

Maria del Morte   No.

Marguerita   I did my tricks . . . snipping dolls . . . the water . . . she did not know . . .

Maria del Morte   No.

Maria   Heaven. Heaven without angels. She remembers nothing . . . her growing up always doing, always saying, always being the wrong *person* . . . She wakes up from a coma and it is like she has just been born! She is *new*! (*She gets up, looks at **Julia**.*) A new mother. (*She sits down beside* **Marguerita**.) Maria del Amor. (*She lies with her head on* **Marguerita**'s *lap*.) Yes.

Marguerita *strokes her hair.*

Julia   Maria!

Maria   Del Amor. It means 'love'.

Julia   Good! Fine! No daughter then . . . I make meals for strangers . . . and . . . the dead!!! (*She goes to the dresser . . . gets a knife.*) Good! Fine! The cord is cut! (*Gets some potatoes.*) I prepare tortilla de patatas for people off the streets and dead souls down from heaven! (*She starts to peel potatoes.*)

Maria del Morte   Meanwhile, seventy miles away, in my home, in my bed, in my mother's arms . . . the new Maria lives.

Marguerita   I sleep next to my daughter.
I comfort her as I would a new-born child.
She is so helpless.
I bathe her . . . I dress her . . . I sing to her.

Sings:

Fear not the wind
Fear not the storm
I have you here
Safe and warm

Maria   Maria Amor Maria . . .

Maria del Morte   This new-born baby cries . . .

Maria   Amor, Maria Amor . . .

Maria del Morte   Ah . . . says everybody . . . the word for love . . . the girl expresses her love for her family!

The two **Marias** *look at each other.* **Maria** *goes to* **Maria del Morte**.

Maria   You were seventeen.

Maria del Morte   Yes.

Maria   I'm seventeen.
(*She reaches out and touches* **Maria del Morte**.) You're so
cold.

Maria del Morte   And it was so hot that day.

Maria   Were you in love?

Maria del Morte   I don't know.

Maria   Were you happy?

Maria del Morte   I don't know.

They smile.

Julia   Maria!

They both look at her.

This . . . is dangerous!

They look back at each other.

Maria del Morte   As I convalesce . . . my family
begin to notice small changes in me . . .

Maria   Small changes?

They both laugh.

Julia   I hope when you are a mother, with children . . .
you find this as funny!

She realises what she has said.

Both Marias   Tragic!

They laugh.

Marguerita   Quiet!!

They become very quiet.

Maria del Morte   My family asks the doctors . . . (*She*

picks up two faces from the newspaper cuttings.) . . . Sasebas
and Perelada . . . about the small changes in me.

Marguerita   Why is her hair darker?

Maria del Morte (*animates one face or cut-out doll*)   It
happens, in illness.

Marguerita   It's coarser . . .

Maria del Morte   Yes. Illness.

Marguerita   And her complexion . . . it seems . . .
rougher . . .

Maria del Morte (*animates another*)   It's the cortizone
injections.

Marguerita   And . . . excuse me . . . someone has
painted her toe-nails . . .

Maria del Morte   Eh? . . . no . . .

Marguerita   And . . . she has metal braces attached to
her teeth . . . and . . . it's a little thing . . . but . . . she
had a mole on her hip . . . and it's not there now . . .

Maria del Morte   My family are working class . . . I
am the first one from these . . . peasants . . . who is
going to university . . . the doctors . . . educated men . . .
see only ignorant peasants . . . Look . . . why do you
care about a little blemish on her hip? . . . These are all
side effects from the drugs we are using to get your
daughter well! The body responding to trauma . . . do
you understand, nnnh?

Marguerita   I'm sorry.

Maria del Morte   My father asks these questions.
Antonio, my brother, asks these questions. My mother
asks no questions, does she?

Marguerita   No.

Maria del Morte   No. She sings lullabies to me with

my small changes! She tends my new-born body!!!

Marguerita   Maria . . . give me peace!!!

Maria del Morte   I can't! I'm in hell!!!

Sings:

> Fear not the wind
> Fear not the storm
> I have you here
> Safe and warm
>
> Fear not the rocks
> The ocean deep
> I hold you close
> Gentle sleep . . .

Singing songs to someone else, comforting someone else
. . . My sister . . . Mari Carmen comes down from
Figueras to see me . . . She looks at me . . . my
coarsened darkened hair . . . my pug nose . . . my
braced teeth . . . and she shouts . . . throughout the
hospital . . . loud enough to wake the dead . . . seventy
miles away in Camas: 'That is not my sister, I don't
care what you say. That is not my sister!!!' And what do
you say to my sister? What do you say to her?

Marguerita   I say . . . Mari Carmen, it is your sister.
You are overcome . . . she is disfigured by the accident
. . . the doctors say the cortizone injections . . . they
know what they are talking about. It is your sister.

Maria *goes to* **Julia**.

Maria   Mama . . . send them away. It scares me.

Julia   Who are you? Why do you call me Mama? I
have no daughter here, do I? My daughter took a new
name . . . for *love* . . . she has a new mother . . . in
Huelva, does she not? My daughter's room is empty.
(*She picks up a newspaper, reads.*) 'Archer Max Hoffman
tried to become a modern-day William Tell when he set

an apple on his son's head. Unfortunately for his son Wolfgang, the shot missed the apple, and went straight through the ten-year-old boy's head, killing him.' Wolfgang Hoffman. Tell me more of your sick daughter, Señora.

Marguerita   She calls me and her father by the words 'Father' and 'Mother' instead of 'Mama' and 'Papa' like always before . . . With Santiago . . . her boyfriend . . . she blows hot and cold . . . sometimes she lets him kiss her . . . other times she shrinks from his touch . . .

Maria   Mama . . . please . . .

Julia   Please? (*She looks away.*)

Maria del Morte (*to* **Maria**)   Please . . . (*She touches* **Maria**.) You are so warm . . . lend me your heart so I can rest in peace.

Maria   How?

Maria del Morte   Make the journey. We will return.

Marguerita   We start to make arrangements for plastic surgery . . . to correct this nose . . . change her face to look like our daughter.

Maria del Morte   They send her to a therapist . . . to speed the recovery of her mind . . . (*She picks up another newspaper picture.*) Enrique Boyer is in his mid-twenties. He has not worked long enough in hospitals to think that all doctors are geniuses . . . all peasants stupid. He has studied psychology at university. He interviews the girl. What is your name?

Maria   Maria.

Maria del Morte (*takes another picture and sits down by* **Maria**)   This is the girl he interviewed.

They both look at the picture.

Maria del Amor. Imagine how she was. Make the

journey. (*She stands up, puts the picture of Enrique Boyer to her face.*) What is your name?

Maria (*puts the picture of **Maria del Amor** to her face*)   Maria del Amor.

Maria del Morte   Maria del Morte.

Maria   Maria del Amor.

Maria del Morte   Maria del Morte.

Maria   No.

Maria del Morte   Yes . . . what is your father's surname?

Maria   Del Morte.

Maria del Morte   What is your mother's surname?

Maria   Del Morte.

Maria del Morte   What is your name?

Maria   Maria del Amor.

Maria del Morte   And where do you live?

Maria   Number twenty-six, Curro Romero Street, Camas.

Maria del Morte   Number three, San Clemente Barrio, Huelva.

Maria   Number twenty-six, Curro Romero Street, Camas.

Maria del Morte   Number three, San Clemente Barrio, Huelva.

Maria   No.

Maria del Morte   Yes. When you leave this office, where do you go to?

Maria   Number three, San Clemente Barrio, Huelva.

Maria del Morte   Do you work?

Maria   I am a student.

Maria del Morte   Of what?

Maria   Of beauty therapy.

Maria del Morte   Of history.

Maria   Of beauty therapy.

Maria del Morte   No.

Maria   Yes.

Maria del Morte   What are the books in your room about?

Maria   History.

Maria del Morte   Tell me about your accident.

Maria   I can't . . .

Maria del Morte   You can. Imagine. Eight-thirty. Hot night.

Maria   Eight-thirty. Hot night.

Maria del Morte   Driving to the beach . . .

Maria   Driving to the beach . . .

Both   The smell of pine through the open window of the car . . . inside of the car hot.

Maria del Morte   I'm thinking of my boy-friend.

Maria   I'm thinking of my girl-friend.

Both   I go into the curve of a long long bend . . . the gravel under the wheels is loose . . . the car bucks . . . skids . . . there's a car coming towards me . . . there's a car coming right at me. The wheel won't turn . . . there's a girl coming at me through the windscreen . . . the windscreen's gone blank . . . it's snow, it's ice, it's burning my face, it's cutting my face, it's in my eyes, into my head, it's slicing my brain into pieces of gravel, what is happening? Where am I? Who am I? I am in pieces all over the road!!

Marguerita   It's eight-thirty.

Julia   Hot night.

Marguerita   My daughter is driving to the beach.

Julia   She said goodbye.

Marguerita   She's always saying goodbye these days . . .

Julia   Can't bear to be in the house . . .

Marguerita   Wants to leave you . . .

Julia   Like you wanted to leave her lots of times, when you had to feed her . . . wipe her face . . . wash her bum . . . play with her . . . clean up her table mess . . . tidy away her toys again and again and again . . .

Marguerita   Everywhere else in the world is more exciting than home . . .

Julia   Everyone else in the world is more exciting than you . . .

Marguerita   She drives off . . . and you think . . . thank God . . . a bit of peace from this . . . stranger called your daughter . . .

Julia   This strange girl who despises what you are . . .

Both   The night darkens . . . it's late . . . she's always later than she says . . . we always have angry words . . . it's very late . . . the anger turns to fear . . . trains collide . . . aeroplanes fall out of the sky . . . mad men lurk in the shadows . . . cars crash.

Marguerita   The telephone rings.

Julia   Who's that at this time of night?

Marguerita   The police.

Julia   The hospital.

Marguerita   Everything you feared.

Julia   Everything you feared for her.

Marguerita   Has happened.

Julia   My daughter.

Marguerita   The nightmare happens.

Both
Fear not the wind
Fear not the storm
I have you here
Safe and warm
Fear not the rocks
The ocean deep
I hold you close
Gently sleep

But in the night, a piper played
Such a tune, of lands unseen
Sunlit forests, mountains high
A winding road, a soaring sky

You dived
You dived

The wind, the storm
The ocean deep
They hold you close
Gently sleep

Maria del Morte   Two families suffer. In Camas, a mother believes her daughter has lost her life. In Huelva, a mother believes her daughter has lost her memory.

Marguerita (*to the two* **Maria**s)   Look . . . (*She takes a newspaper and begins tearing it.*) There was once a land with no trees.

Maria del Morte *smiles in recognition.*

Marguerita And it was very hot ... and the people had no shade. (*She keeps tearing.*) So they went to the wisest old woman of the land and said 'Make us a tree'. (*She keeps tearing.*) So she did. (*She starts pulling from the centre of the newspaper and out comes a newspaper palm tree.*) She made them a tree. (*She pulls out some more.*) And it grew and grew and grew. (*It grows and grows and grows.*) Until she had made them a very tall tree. And all the people of the land were happy.

Maria del Morte *claps,* **Maria** *does not.*

Marguerita Here ... (*She gives the tree to* **Maria**.)

Maria del Morte The mother in Huelva tries to remind her daughter of the past ...

Marguerita Don't you remember the tree story? Don't you remember the tree? You must remember all the trees I made ...

Maria del Morte She begs ...

Marguerita When you were a little girl ... you were always saying ...

Maria del Morte Make me a tree to sleep under ...

Marguerita Make me a tree to sleep under ...

Maria del Morte But the new Maria does not remember the tree ...

Maria I remember another tree ... (*To* **Julia**.) Do you remember the picnic we had at the Fluvia?

Julia In your yellow dress ...

Maria That you said I shouldn't wear because I would spoil it ...

Julia It was your newest dress ... for a picnic ...

Maria   And I cried and cried . . .

Julia   You shrieked and yelled . . .

Maria   And finally you said . . .

Julia   'God in Heaven . . . if it's so important, wear the bloody dress . . . but don't blame me if anything happens to it!!!'

Maria   And I went to the River Fluvia in my new yellow dress.

Julia   And I went to the River Fluvia in a stinking temper!

Maria   And I climbed that tree . . .

Julia   Overhanging the River Fluvia . . .

Maria   And the branch was slippy and I . . .

Julia   Fell splash into the River Fluvia.

Maria   And you waded in and fished me out . . .

Julia   So we both got soaked in the River Fluvia!

Maria   And then Mama . . .

Julia   And then I looked at you . . . your yellow dress . . . *khaki* . . . with the mud of Fluvia and me . . . khaki with the mud of Fluvia . . . and I laughed and laughed and laughed . . .

Maria   Yes. It's the same thing now, Mama.

Julia   No.

Maria   Yes. Let me put on my yellow dress because I'm happy. Let me climb the trees because I am well and happy.

Julia   And if you *fall*!!!

Maria   Let me fall!!!

Julia   Into this stinking disgusting mud which will

cover us all . . .

Maria   Laugh at it! Look at me and laugh . . . because I am happy!!!

Julia   Listen to me . . . just as I waded into the river and dragged you from the mud of Fluvia . . . so will I wade in and drag you from this mud you wallow in now!!!

Maria   Aaaaagh! (*She flings the paper tree at* **Julia**.)

Maria del Morte   What would you have felt, Mother . . . if I had fallen in love with a girl?

Marguerita   I would have felt as she felt. No mother wants this pain for her daughter.

Maria del Morte   Or joy either? Enrique Boyer, our therapist, is confused. His patient, Maria, grows physically stronger every day. But what, oh what of her mind? She lives . . . in Huelva. (*She draws its position in the dust.*) Her name is Maria del Morte . . . But why, oh why, does she insist on calling herself Maria del Amor . . . and giving her address as Camas . . . seventy miles away and in a different province? (*She draws its position in the dust.*) Why does a girl from here . . . Huelva . . . a student of history in Huelva . . . know the telephone number of a bar of a beautician's school in Seville? (*Draws in Seville . . . studies the puzzle.*) He is puzzled. How can he explain it? He decides to go back to the start, to the accident . . . He searches out the accident report and discovers that it took place at Punta Umbria . . . midway between Camas and Huelva . . . and discovers that the driver of one car was Maria del Morte, the driver of the other car Maria del Amor who lived in Camas, who now lies buried in the cemetery in Camas. Why has Maria del Morte taken on the details of the dead girl's life? What is your name?

Maria   Mud.

Maria del Morte   Where do you live?

Maria   Here. There. Nowhere.

Maria del Morte   What is your mother's name?

No answer from **Maria**.

Maria del Morte   What is your father's name?

No answer from **Maria**.

Maria del Morte   Tell me about your accident . . .

Maria   Leave me alone . . .

Maria del Morte   Perhaps, thinks Boyer, the girl has overheard the name of Maria del Amor, the address of Maria del Amor, in the confusion after the accident . . . What do you remember of your accident?

Maria   I was not in this accident!

Maria del Morte   His theory takes hold.

Maria   There's a river that flows . . . and . . . you're little . . . and it seems a long way across to the other bank . . . so . . . you stay on your own side . . . the water up to your ankles . . . and then you go in a bit deeper . . . to your knees . . . and the current flows past you . . . pulling your legs . . . up to your waist . . . up to your chest . . . and all the time . . . the other bank gets closer . . . until one day . . . you're swimming . . . and you could do it . . . you could reach the other side . . . but by then . . . you can swim . . . and the current's pulling you the other way . . . downstream . . . because that way's longer . . . rivers are longer than they are wide . . . and you want to go that way . . . not across to the other bank . . .

Maria del Morte   Enrique Boyer, with his incomplete knowledge, believes that her sanity is flowing away . . .

Maria   I'll swim.

Julia Against the current! It's hard swimming against the current . . .

Maria I'm swimming the way I want . . .

Julia It's the wrong way!!!

Maria del Morte Enrique Boyer reluctantly considers the use of electric shock.

Maria Nooooo!!!! (*Takes newspaper and reads.*) 'Two sisters, aged twelve and nineteen, who were kept captive almost all of their lives by their mother, have been freed. The mother, widow Maria Kolb, 48, feared the girls would catch some disease in the outside world. The elder girl, Eva, had spent only six days at primary school, and her sister, Heidi-Marie, had never been to one. The only time they escaped from their home in Bayreuth, Bavaria, was several years ago when their grandmother took them shopping while their mother was out. Police said Mrs Kolb threatened to kill the girls and herself when they went to free them. They found a loaded revolver under a cushion in her living room. The girls looked dazed when taken from their home.'
Looked dazed, looked dazed, looked dazed, Maria Kolb, Eva Kolb, Heidi-Marie Kolb. (*She goes down on her knees and starts writing in the dust.*)

Maria del Morte *stands and looks at what she is writing.*

Maria del Morte (*reads*) 'To what there is . . . there is . . . what there isn't' . . . to what there is there is what there isn't . . . Enrique Boyer took the girl's scribbling as a plea for help . . .

Maria Help me . . . somebody please help me . . . please, please, somebody help me . . .

Maria del Morte Enrique Boyer decided to try another tack.

Marguerita *takes a small book from her bag, and shows it to* **Julia**.

Marguerita   Dictionary. I have lately been looking up the meaning of words . . .

Maria del Morte   Boyer came from Catalunya . . . in the far north of Spain . . .

Marguerita   I need to know *exactly* what the words mean . . . do you understand?

Maria del Morte   In the opposite corner from Andalucia . . . where now he worked . . .

Marguerita   Words such as love . . . such as death . . . such as mother . . . do you know?

Maria del Morte   But as it happened . . . one of the few people he knew in Andalucia was a doctor from Camas . . .

Marguerita   When they say 'She is dead' . . . I need to know what that means . . .

Maria del Morte   The doctor was his friend. It was an extraordinary coincidence.

Marguerita   Coincidence. (*Starts looking up the word.*) Two girls . . . seventeen . . . in two cars . . . named Maria . . . meet in the same terrible moment . . . (*Reads.*) 'a chance occurrence of events . . . remarkable for apparently being connected . . .'

Maria del Morte   'It was an extraordinary coincidence' said Boyer . . . Camas is a very small town . . . and Spain a very big country!

Marguerita   What is an accident? Why my daughter? Why her?

Maria del Morte   Enrique Boyer asks his doctor to come and look at Maria del Morte. Perhaps he will understand why the girl keeps calling 'Amor Amor'. The doctor looks at the girl. He stares. He goes outside. Leans against the wall. 'But this girl is Maria del Amor, Curro Romero Street, Camas,' he says. 'This is Maria del Amor!'

Marguerita *starts crying.*

Maria del Morte   The doctor from Camas goes back to the little town . . . he tells Toni Reina . . . the girl's aunt . . .

Marguerita   Like spies . . . traitors . . . behind my back . . . the doctors plot . . .

Maria del Morte   Toni Reina comes to the clinic at Huelva . . .

Marguerita   I let her go to the clinic because I thought they were mending her . . .

Maria del Morte   Toni Reina looks at her niece. 'Do you know who I am?' she asks. Maria del Amor nods calmly.

Marguerita   How could she *know?*

Maria del Morte   Toni Reina tells the Mayor of Camas. They start to collect evidence to reclaim the daughter of their town. Frequently, the mayor meets the parents of Maria del Amor on the street . . . he cannot sleep for he is weighted down with his secret.

Marguerita   No one told me this was happening! Behind my back.

Maria del Morte   Then the mayor tells the parents of Maria del Amor. It is arranged for the father to see Maria del Amor in the Huelva clinic.

Marguerita   Still nobody tells us!

Maria del Morte   The father looks at the girl. He is in anguish. He wants to shout . . . to take her in his arms . . . to hold her safe. Maria del Amor registers no surprise at seeing her father. She smiles. She puts her finger to her lips and says 'Shhh. Otherwise they'll leave me here.'

Marguerita   Shhh. Otherwise they'll leave me here.

Maria del Morte   Maria del Amor's father goes to the police to demand the return of his daughter. What did this family want with his daughter? How could they not know that Maria del Amor was not their child?

Marguerita   All this time . . . I am letting her go to the clinic, believing they are making her well. My husband is called in. He is shown photograph albums of the girl. He tells my son Antonio . . . 'It's not your sister . . . it's someone else . . . I have seen an album full of photographs of the girl' . . . It all becomes clear to them . . . all the doubts . . . the painted toe-nails . . . the missing mark on her thigh . . . so. So . . . my family do not have the courage to tell me the truth . . . they say Maria is needed for urgent tests . . . and my husband escorts her round the corner . . . where her father waits with two police officers. And on August the first . . . for the second time . . . my daughter is taken away from me forever.

There is silence.

Julia   How could you not know that she was not yours?

No answer.

Marguerita *takes a newspaper and starts to tear it.*

Julia   For seventeen years you held this girl . . . you fed her at your breast . . . you looked with wonder on her every day . . . knowing she was yours . . . when she fell down . . . you kissed her face and rubbed her knee and saw that she was better . . . when she cried . . . *you* hurt . . . when she screamed . . . you felt the pain in *your* heart . . . when she fell into danger . . . you were gripped at the throat with fear . . . How could you not know that she was not your child???

Marguerita *says nothing. She continues tearing her newspaper.*

Julia And somewhere . . . all this time . . . was a mother . . . just like you . . . feeling as you felt . . . sitting in a dark room . . . lit by one lamp . . . staring into the night . . . thinking no thought but this . . . my daughter is dead . . . I cannot understand it . . . my daughter is dead! How could you do it? (*She goes to* **Maria**.) Maria . . . whatever you are . . . whatever I am . . . I know one thing . . . you are my daughter . . . and I love you more than life. Let us go into the house and I will block your door shut with a chair so that ghosts cannot come and take you.

Maria Mama. No. What you fear for me can't be held by a chair against a door. A thousand chairs against a thousand doors will not keep it out. Something has come and taken me. The ghosts are here.

Maria del Morte My body was dug up and brought back from Camas to Huelva. I was returned to my family. My parents were too upset to identify me. They asked my brother, Antonio, to look at me . . . see that it was me. After two months in the coffin . . . my looks had gone. I had decomposed badly. My skin had blackened. The smell was nauseous. But Antonio could recognise me instantly. 'It was horrible,' he says. 'When I see a photograph of my sister now, or when I talk about her, the image of her all black inside the coffin comes back to me. I can't get rid of it.' He does not sleep now . . . for I can come through a thousand doors. (*She smiles.*) The one advantage of being dead. I may visit where I please . . . whenever I please . . .

Sings.

A thousand chairs
Against a thousand doors
A thousand doors
In a thousand walls
Will not keep me away
I will come to you

A thousand keys
Turned in a thousand locks
A thousand links
In a thousand chains
Will not keep me away
I will come to you . . .

Maria *stands and watches* **Marguerita** *tearing her paper.*

Maria   Señora, what are you doing?

Marguerita   Tearing newspaper.

Maria   Señora . . . how could you not know that it was not your daughter?

Marguerita   How could I not know.
This is a question I have been asked a thousand times . . .
How could I not know?
Asked by the police . . .
How could I not know?
Asked by the neighbours . . .
How could I not know?
Asked by my children . . .
How could I not know?
Asked by the newspapers . . . every newspaper in all of Spain . . . Señora . . . but how . . . excuse me . . . a few words . . . for our readers . . . for the public . . . how could you not know that this girl was not your daughter?

Maria del Morte   I cannot rest . . . I cannot sleep . . . I cannot lie down in my blackened, stinking, decomposing body in the graveyard in Huelva . . . until my mind is at peace . . . Mother . . . how could you not know that it wasn't me???

Marguerita *touches her daughter's face.* **Maria del Morte** *does nothing.*

Marguerita   In Camas . . . a daughter believed dead

was returned to her mother. The newspapers are filled
with stories of the girl's reunion with her parents. A
television programme names her 'Andalucian of the
Year'. Camino, the matador, dedicates the killing of a
bull to her in the Seville bull-ring. A film company want
to make a film version of her story. There is much
rejoicing . . . that a daughter, believed dead, was
returned to her mother.

Maria del Morte On All Souls' Day . . . Maria . . .
the living Maria . . . asks her parents to take her to see
her crypt in Camas cemetery. The crypt in which my
body lay for two months. She said 'I want to discover
something of that other world.' She stood before her
empty tomb and laughed. (*To* **Maria**.) Wouldn't you?

Maria Yes.

Maria del Morte Glad to be alive.

Maria Yes.

Marguerita A daughter returned from the dead. Yes,
I would laugh too. If I could have my daughter returned
from the dead . . . I would do anything . . . I would care
for her as a new-born baby . . . I would sleep next to
her and comfort her . . .
I would take the paint off her toe-nails. I would say
'There was no mark on her thigh' . . . I would have her
nose changed by plastic surgery . . . I would send volt
after volt through her brain until she *was* my Maria!!!

She pulls out the newspaper. It is a long, long ladder.

Julia Oh God!

Marguerita My daughter was dead . . . I tried to
build a ladder so I could climb to hell and get her . . .
How could I not know that this Maria was not mine? I
knew! I knew the first day it wasn't my daughter. How
could I not? (*Pause.*) But . . . I couldn't bring myself to
let her go.

There is complete silence.

Maria   What if ... the electric shock treatment had ... had worked ... what if she ... the girl ... had never remembered who she really was?

Marguerita   I don't know. I was found out. It is in all the newspapers. I am infamous.

Maria del Morte   Mama. It is time you went home. There is a family there who loves you. There is a grave to tend in Huelva in which lies the body of your daughter. Go home ... Let the newspapers write that there lives a mother who loved her daughter so much. The one advantage of a dead daughter is that she can visit where she pleases ... when she pleases ... I will come through a thousand doors to you to the end of your life. And then, perhaps, you will come to me. (*She goes.*)

The two women and the girl sit.

Maria   It's cold.

Julia   The sun's gone. (*She shivers.*) Señora ... it's time I made supper ... come in and sit by the cooker while I make some nice hot tortillas de patatas ... mmm?

Marguerita   I must go home.

Julia   Eat first.

Marguerita   I'm not hungry.

Maria   I am.

Marguerita   Good. Eat it up. Every scrap.

She stands, collects her bag and possessions.

Marguerita   Eating her supper now ... is a girl also called Maria. Her broken ankle is mended, the scars on her face have healed, her memory has returned. She remembers the accident. She remembers nothing of the time she spent with me. I am very happy about this.

I'm not her mother, you see. I lay my hand upon the forehead of this house. Let it be free of pain. (*She goes.*)

Pause.

Julia Well. Tortilla de patatas.

Maria Mmm . . . yes . . .

Julia Tomato salad . . .

Maria Oh . . . yes . . .

Julia And . . . a little chorizo!

Maria And a lot of chorizo!

Julia Right then! (*She gets up with her peeled potatoes, halfway to the house, she stops.*) Did that . . . just then . . .

Maria No! Don't say . . . Pretend we read it in the newspapers.

Julia Right. Right then. (*She goes a quarter of the way to the house. She stops.*) After supper . . .

Maria What?

Julia You're not going out, I suppose . . .

Maria I don't know.

Julia It'll be late . . .

Maria Not that late.

Julia But you won't be going out . . .

Maria I might.

Julia I don't think you should, not tonight.

Maria Well . . . I might not. I'll see.

Julia You'll see.

Maria Probably not. I'll see.

Julia Well after tortilla and tomato salad and chorizo

... I'd just be too full to move!

Maria   Mmm ... I know ...

She stretches on a bench, as if there for life.

Julia   Right! Tortilla de patatas.

Goes into the house singing ...

Fear not the wind
Fear not the storm
I have you here
Safe and warm

Maria *listens to her mother singing.*

Maria   Here's what I'm going to do tonight. After
supper ... I'm going to put on my ... blue dress ...
yes ... and I'll go to ... to Felipe's because ... because
they play good music ... and everybody'll be there ...
and ... Paula ... she'll be there ... and we'll all have
a good time ... we'll dance with the boys ... Pepe ...
and Juan-Carlos ... and Michelito ... and then ...
we'll get in Paula's car ... just Paula and me ... and
we'll drive with the windows open so we can smell the
pine ... through the woods ... by the *twisty* road ...
down to the beach for a swim. And when we're in the
water ... I might, I just might get hold of Paula ...
and kiss her dead on the lips! Yes!

As she makes up she sings.

A thousand chairs
Against a thousand doors
A thousand doors
In a thousand walls
Will not keep me away
I will come to you.

A thousand keys
Turned in a thousand locks
A thousand links

In a thousand chains
Will not keep me away
I will come to you

Julia (*from within the house*)   Maria!

Maria   What?

Julia   Supper!

Maria *goes into the house.*

Her Aching Heart

Her Aching Heart was first performed by the Women's
Theatre Group at the Oval House, London, on 23 May
1990 with the following cast:

Harriet	
Lady Harriet Helstone	Nicola Kathrens
Granny	
Joshua	
Molly	
Molly Penhallow	Sarah Kevney
Betsy	
Lord Rothermere	

Directed by Claire Grove
Designed by Amanda Fisk
Music written by Juliet Hill
Music arranged by Juliet Hill, Janette Mason and Ros
Mason
Lighting by Lizz Poulter

Act One

A Broken-Hearted Woman Sings

There is a woman. Her name is **Harriet**. *She is broken-hearted.*
She sings.

Song: Uninvited

Harriet
After too many cigarettes
After too much gin
When I think 'I'll go to bed'
That's when you come in
You creep into my mind
And say 'Hello'
Babe . . . you weren't invited
Please will you go?

I didn't invite you
Didn't ask you my dear
Babe . . . you're unwelcome
So why are you here?

After I've played too many tracks
After too much sound
When I think 'that's quite enough'
That's when you call round
You steal into my heart
And say 'Hello'
Babe . . . you weren't invited
Please will you go?

I didn't invite you
Thought I'd made it clear
Babe . . . you're unwelcome
So why are you here?

After I've picked out a good book
After thumbing through

When I think 'bedtime reading'
The words all say 'you'
You crawl into my head
And say 'Hello'
Babe . . . you weren't invited
Please will you go?

I didn't invite you
Thought I'd made it clear
Babe . . . you're unwelcome
So why are you here?

She sighs, mooches around, picks up a book, looks at the cover.

Harriet (*reads*) 'Her Aching Heart.' (*She laughs wrily.*) 'A lesbian historical romance.' (*She sighs, opens the book, reads.*) 'Last night I dreamt I went to Helstone Hall again. It seemed to me I stood before the intricately-wrought iron gate leading to the densely-wooded drive, and for a while I could not enter for the way was barred to me.' (*She laughs wrily, stands up, collects what she needs to, reads.*) 'There was a lock and chain keeping shut the gate.'

Reading still, she exits. As she does, the book itself opens up and we are inside it.

Chapter One: A Nun Has A Nightmare

A woman enters, dressed in a shift. Her heart is aching. Anguish clouds her sweet eyes.

Molly Last night I dreamt I went to Helstone Hall again. It seemed to me I stood before the intricately-wrought iron gate leading to the densely-wooded drive, and for a while I could not enter for the way was barred to me. There was a lock and chain keeping shut the gate. I called in my dream to the lodge-keeper . . . crusty, kindly Samuel, 'Helloooo! Let me by!' But no answer came and peering through the rusted rococo I saw that Samuel's cheery cottage was empty. No smoke curled from the chimney. No smell of baking bread issued from the gaping door. No comfort met me.

Then, like all dreamers, I was possessed of a sudden with supernatural powers ... and I passed like a spirit through the gate and was racing, like a thing possessed, up the twisting drive. Past the gnarled oaks choked with ivy. Past the rhododendron bushes twisted and tortured. Past the bracken rank and wild. And I stood before the mighty, looming presence of Helstone Hall.

She clutches at her heart.

Oooooooh! Dear Watcher, it was EMPTY!!!!! The Great Lawn, once smooth and green as a billiard table ... was tossed and torn with mole-mounds ... The soaring grey-granite walls were choked and poked with thrusting tendrils of ivy ... The mullioned windows, once twinkling with bubbled bright glass, were broken, dark ... like blinded eyes. Helstone Hall was an empty shell, just as is now my breast where once beat my gentle heart.

Her tears flow, like the River Dart, fast and furious. She picks up a black garment, wipes her eyes upon it. She puts it on.

Moonlight can play odd tricks upon the fancy ... for in my dream, excitement rippled through my slight form ... and I could swear the house was not empty ... but pulsed with life ... Pungent woodsmoke puffed from the myriad chimney pots, warm light from many-branched silver candlesticks streamed from the windows and the warm night air carried the sound of human voices.

There is the sound of human voices.

The wild and extravagant Helstones down from London with their rakish friends ... the rich and dissolute men, (*She puts on a white close-fitting hood.*) the beautiful powdered women (*She puts on a cross.*) and at the centre of that glittering throng, rich and lovely, ardent and wilful, the impetuous Lady Harriet Helstone. (*She puts on a wimple.*)

Harriet. (*With warm affection.*) Harriet. (*With lust.*) Harriet. (*With longing.*) Harriet. (*With hatred.*) Harriet. (*With emptiness.*) Harriet.

She picks up a bible and exits.

Chapter Two: A Lady Attends To Her Toilet

The sound of human voices continues. A woman enters in historical underwear. She is beautiful, wild, wilful and wearily discontented.

Harriet   Oh how *weary* I am of our rakish friends! How tired I am of rich and dissolute men! How fatigued I am with beautiful and powdered women! Small wonder I am ardent and wilful! Small wonder London society is agog with my outrageous pranks. Little wonder that a devil of discontent mars my otherwise lovely countenance!

She stares at the devil of discontent reflected in her chevalier glass.

What do these laughing grey eyes look for? What will warm these rose-petalled cheeks? What can quicken the lips of this generous mouth? I let Rothermere steal a kiss last night.

She sighs discontentedly.

'Twas tiresome! Tralala ... what care I if the servants talk, if Mama looks cross, if Papa threatens to take me still across his knee ... even though I have put up my hair and been received in Polite Society!!! Where is Betsy? I want to get dressed!!!

Rings a bell.

Not here! ... I'll beat the scamp! Very well ... I'll dress myself! Ah ... my riding habit!

She puts it on.

How well it fits my magnificent figure. I'll cut a dash in

the field today! Ah ... my boots! Polished with a secret concoction of boot-blackening and champagne known only to my father's gentleman! Ah ... my hat! I'll set it at a rakish angle to show off its Parisienne millinery! There!

She picks up a riding crop. Stares at herself in the glass.

Harriet. Today's the hunt. Mount your black stallion Thunderer ... the one Papa says is too strong for a lady ... (*She laughs.*) Call your dogs ... Jasper! ... Judas! ... Julian! ... Follow the fox! (*We hear the sounds of horses, dogs.*) Lose yourself in the hunt!!!

A horn blows. **Harriet** *exits.*

Another Broken-Hearted Woman Sings A Song

Molly *comes on in modern dress. She is reading* Her Aching Heart.

Molly   'And it seemed to me in my dream, that when I called her name I was no longer a votive nun dedicated to prayers, humility and chastity ... and growing God's greenery in my beloved monastery garden ... but was transported back in time ... as can happen in dreams ... to that day I first encountered ... her ...'

She sighs. She mooches around. She sings.

Song: Heart Surgery

Molly
   Gave it up
   Loving
   Bad for my heart
   Gave it up
   Feeling
   Tore me apart

Should have read the warning
'Loving can seriously damage your health'
But it's an addiction
And creeps up by stealth

Well, doctor
You had my heart in your hand
That's why there's blood on your sleeve
Well, doctor
The operation hurt me
But that's normal I believe

Gave it up
Loving
Bad for my heart
Gave it up
Feeling
Tore me apart

Heart surgery
All for the best
Left me with just
This machine ticking away in my breast

She sighs, mooches around, picks up the book again, reads.

'Harriet. Her name spoke in my heart. Harriet!'

Harriet . . . (*She finds a piece of cigarette packet in her pocket. She reads the telephone number on it.*) 'Harriet . . . 071 294 6033.' Mmm . . . Harriet.

She exits as **Harriet** *enters.*

Harriet (*in riding habit*)   What a fresh, fine, sharp Cornish morning. I declare . . . it lifts my heart like a sparrow . . . tossing it in winged joy on gently-wafting currents of air! The trees rustle in the light wind! The sun streaks like a basset hound across the fields! The sea gallops like a thoroughbred mare pounding its shiny hooves upon the rocks along the shore! Oh what a day! Oh what a wind of hope blows through the echoing

corridors of my breast! rattling at the knobs and
knockers of the doors to my dry and dusty emotions! I
shall flush some wild game from the hedgerows and
chase it far this morn! To the Hunt!!!!!

Hunting horns. Hooves. Hounds.

Chapter Three: Thorns

*A briar and bramble thicket on the wilder reaches of the Helstone
estate. The nun enters . . . She is dressed as a young village
maiden. She is unaware of this.*

Molly   And it seemed to me, in my dream, that when
I called her name . . . I was no longer a votive nun . . .
I was again that simple, untried eighteen-year-old village
maiden . . . with that clear translucent skin.

*She puts her hand up to her face and is shocked to feel that it is
clear and translucent.*

Aaaaaaah!!! Wearing my simple rough holland gown.

*She puts her hands to her breast and is shocked to feel that it is
covered with simple rough holland material.*

Aaaaaaah!!!

She looks down and sees how she is dressed.

I was again picking blackberries in a briar and bramble
thicket on the wilder reaches of the Helstone estate . . .

She sees the thorn bushes.

Aaaaaaaaaaaaah!!!!! How strong the dream is! It is as if
. . . I could reach out . . . and feel the prick of the thorn
on my finger . . .

She reaches out and feels the prick of the thorn on her finger.

Ooooooooow!!! It is as if . . . I could pick a blackberry
. . . put it in my mouth . . . and taste its soft sweetness!

She picks a blackberry . . . puts it in her mouth . . . and tastes its soft sweetness. We hear the baying of hounds, the horn, the thundering of hooves. She is eighteen again.

(*Suddenly alert.*) What was that? (*She listens.*) Why . . . it's the Helstone Hunt! Coming this way! I must away before they catch me on their land!!! Rumour has it that the Helstones *thrash* common folk found on their demesne!

Suddenly, a fox races on.

A fox! Ah, poor hunted beast! I'll save you.

She picks up the fox. It is quivering with fright.

Oh, poor thing . . . you're quivering with fright! What can we do? I'll take you home to my poor but specklessly clean cottage . . . Oh no . . . my gown is caught on the thorn bush! I'm trapped! Oh no!!!!

The baying of hounds, the horn, the thundering of hooves reaches a crescendo. Offstage we hear . . .

Harriet (*off*) Hold your horses! Hold them I say! Curb
those hounds! Curb them I say! The fox has gone to ground in this dense copse of thorns!!! I'll dismount . . . here . . . hold Thunderer . . . I'll beat a way through with my riding crop and flush out Wily Reynard!!! No no . . . I'll go on my own!

Harriet *enters, mud-splashed and glowing.*

Now, where are you . . . you pointed-snouted murderer of poultry? AaaaH!

She stops short.

God's Wounds! What have we here? A Trespasser. A Peasant by the look of that rough holland gown. But why all a-quiver! Hare an' Hounds! She holds my fox!!!!

She is understandably furious.

Girl . . . peasant . . . underling . . . you interrupt my

hunt! Let go the fox!

Molly   Madam . . . I will not.

Harriet   You will not? Madam . . . come here to me!

Molly   Madam I cannot.

Harriet   You cannot? Madam . . . I am Gentry . . .
have you taken leave of your senses?

Molly   Madam . . . I have not.

Harriet   Will not . . . cannot . . . have not . . . You are
all nots! And so you will be if I tie you hand and foot
and beat the nots out of you, you will be knots indeed!!!

Molly   Madam . . . I *will* not for all my life I have
loved the creatures of the field and wood and they,
responding, all come to me with broken wings, sore
paws, dislocated ears . . . Madam . . . I *cannot* for I am
trapped in this thorny spot by sharp briars. Madam . . .
I *have* not for I know you will not kill this fox!

Harriet   Why will I not kill the fox, you impudent
girl?

Molly   For within your breast, Madam, beats a
woman's heart.

Harriet   Wrong, Madam! I have no heart at all! Ask
any man in London! I am the wilful Lady Harriet
Helstone and I take what I want and the fox is mine!

Molly   Lady Harriet Helstone . . . ?

Harriet   Yes!

Molly   . . . of Helstone Hall . . . ?

Harriet   Yes!

Molly   . . . of the hellraising Helstones . . . ?

Harriet   Yes.

Molly   Madam . . . let me go.

Harriet   Madam I will.

Harriet *kneels to release* **Molly***'s gown.*

Molly (*looking down in wondering surprise on* **Harriet***'s elegant riding hat*)   She releases me . . .

Harriet (*looking down in wondering surprise on* **Molly***'s shabby holland gown*)   I release her . . .

They look into each other's countenances for what seems like an aeon. At the same time, both shake their heads as if they are dismissing an almighty and unwelcome thought.

Harriet   I let you go . . . But I will take the fox!

Molly   No!!!

Harriet   Yes!!!

Molly   See how he quivers!!!

Harriet   You both quiver!!!

They do.

Molly   He with fright . . . I with passion!!!!!!!!!!!! Look into his eyes . . . see how they roll in terror! Observe his sharp teeth rigid in a rictus of fear! See his proud tail bushy and upstanding with fright! Understand the determination which courses like *Fire* through every fibre of my being! You will not kill this fox!!!

Harriet   And understand the wilfulness which storms like a *Tornado* through every fibre of *my* being! I will kill this fox!!!

Molly   You *indescribable monster*!!!!

Harriet   You *unconscionable upstart*!!! The fox goes with me!

Molly   The fox stays!

The fox takes an active interest in this exchange.

Harriet   I have a riding whip!

Molly   I have sharp teeth. So does the fox!

Harriet   I will beat you until you are black and blue!

Molly   I will bite you until *you* are black and blue. And so will the fox.

Harriet   I will beat you until your rough holland gown is as thin as silk!

Molly   I will bite you until your magnificent riding habit hangs in tatters and rags! And so will the fox.

Harriet   I will take you to my opulent bed and there on the fine satin sheets I will kiss your lips with such intention that I will kiss out your soul . . .

Molly   I will take you to my truckle bed and there on the simple cotton sheet I will touch your body with such intention that I will bring forth your soul . . .

Harriet   What?

Molly   What?

Surely they both misheard.

Harriet   I misheard.

Molly   I misheard. So did the fox. I am going to set down the fox . . . and you are going to let him escape . . .

Harriet   Try it!

Molly   I do. See. (*She sets down the fox.*) Run, Reynard. (*Oddly enough, it doesn't.*)

Harriet   Run, Reynard. (*She hits it with her riding crop.*) Escape, fool!!!

Sadly, this makes the fox run in the wrong direction . . . towards the hunt.

Molly   Oh yes!

Harriet   Oh no!

There is a baying of hounds, a thundering of hooves, a horn, excited cries.

Molly   Oh no!

Harriet   No ... no ... no ... no ... NOOOOOOOO! (*She hurries off.*)

Molly   No ... oh ... no ... please ... no ... no ... NOOOOOOOOOO!!!

There is a bloodcurdling, fox-like scream. **Molly** *collapses, weeping.*

Harriet *returns with her hands covered in blood.*

Harriet   Too late. Poor Reynard. I ...

Molly   Enough! (*She wipes away her tears, for she is too proud, though but a lowly peasant, to let the* **Lady Harriet** *see her cry. She sees the blood on* **Harriet**'s *hands.*) Aaaaaah! Blood!

Harriet   Yes ... I ...

Molly   Enough! Murderer! Assassin! Savage! Do not sully these green woods with your red red words!

Harriet   But ... Madam ... I ...

Molly   Silence! Never speak to me again! Never open your mouth again in my presence! Never come near me again! From the first moment I set eyes on you, I have hated you from the very bottom of my heart! Lady Harriet Helstone ... I call down a curse on you! May the blood that this day you have shed of this innocent fox be repaid a hundred nay a thousand times. May the Helstone blood flow like a storm-swollen river through your halls. May it flow to the sea and wash, wash away the family of Helstone from the memory of all humanity! May your family never prosper, never be happy, never be merry. May you never marry! May you never ever ever *ever* hunt again!!!

She exits.

Harriet   Damn you . . . I tried! I went against my
blood, my class, my lineage, my character to save that
wretched fox! I flung myself, uncaring of my favourite
riding habit before M'father, M'mother, M'brother's
mounts. Painted, powdered Lady Adelia Beasley smirked
. . . 'What's this . . . a damn lily-liver?' 'No, not that,
never that' I cried. But they let loose the dogs . . .
canine mouths slavered, canine mouths opened . . . shut
. . . tore that fox from my very arms and . . . and . . .
and Thunder And Lightning!!! It was but a Paltry
Fox!!!! Jervis . . . bring Thunderer about . . . I would
ride away!!!!

There is a sound of thundering hooves, whinnies. She exits.

Hold him still! Kneel down Jervis! Without a mounting
stool I must needs use your back!

The hooves canter away.

Chapter Four: A Buxom Young Wench and A Sprightly Old Woman

Two scenes now unfold simultaneously. The first is **Lady
Harriet***'s dressing room, the second is the cheery, simple but
specklessly clean cottage where* **Molly** *lives.*

Lady Harriet *enters the first scene.*

Harriet   God's Wounds!! Hare 'n' Hounds!! Thunder
'n' Turf! What a *vile* humour possesses me . . . Betsy!
Come and change me! Where is that demn gel?

Betsy *enters. Although in these penurious times she may seem
physically similar to* **Molly Penhallow** *. . . she is a*
completely different *character. Born in Cheapside, she is a pert
member of the serving classes.*

Betsy   Here I am, Mum! Lawks-a-mercy, Milady, look

how you've a-ruined your grand gown! I'm sure I don't know how I'm to sponge and mop all the blood and mud out of that fine raiment to be sure!

Harriet   Silence, babbler! Curb your pert tongue and busy yourself with pulling off my boots!

Betsy   Yes, Mum! Mercy, Milady . . . how tight they are! Tight as a tinker's trailer and no mistake! I need the strength of ten costermongers for this task and no mistake!

She pulls off the boots.

Harriet   Mistake . . . mistake? I have had enough of mistakes today . . . so hold your tongue!

Betsy   Yes, Milady! There, Milady! Off in a trice!

Harriet   Undo me!

Betsy   Yes, Mum! (*She undoes* **Lady Harriet**.) I'll take these dirty boots to the boot boy, Milady . . . he's out there a-collecting the ladies' and gentlemen's boots of all the ladies' and gentlemen's ladies and gentlemen!

She exits.

Harriet   I am wild with rage! See how my breast heaves! Feel how my heart pounds! My skin burns with fury!

As her jacket is undone, we can probably see all this.

That girl! That ridiculous, stupid, ignorant, uneducated, untitled girl! Where did she go? How dare she leave before I dismissed her? How dare she dash away to . . . where . . . a hovel I suppose . . . a nasty, low, dirty cote in the village I suppose . . . I suppose there is a village down there in the valley . . . I suppose she is there even now . . . surrounded by her low folk . . . telling her snivelling tale . . .

As **Harriet** *muses in her splendid room* **Molly** *enters her* *specklessly clean cottage.*

Molly Ah, home at last! Granny! Oh, Granny dearest
... I'm home! Where is she? Out gathering faggots I
daresay, for our supper fire! I'll see if I can spy her
from the window!

Meanwhile ...

Harriet Oh, I cannot sit still! Where is that girl??? I
will go and pace my room until she returns!

She exits.

Meanwhile ...

Molly No, nowhere to be seen ... it's perhaps as well
... there is such turmoil in my heart that I must calm
its storms or dear old Granny will be tossed on my
inner seas! That lady! That rude, cruel, arrogant,
overweening, proud lady! How could she? How could
she kill my fox friend? I expect she has mounted her
horse ... and ridden off up that high hill ... to where?
... to Helstone Hall I suppose ... and she is sitting
there now with all her mighty and powerful friends ...
laughing at my plight ... sneering at my red-haired
friend's death ... Oh Granny, there you are.

Although in these penurious times it may seem that **Granny**
looks not unlike **Lady Harriet**, *she is in fact a completely
different character, being a cheery, nut-cheeked, wise old villager
who, unlike her granddaughter, speaks in simple peasant vernacular.*

Molly Ah, you have found some faggots for the fire!

Granny Oh yes my little nutkin! I been by the
hedgerows and ditchrows a-foraging and a-faggoting.
And regard ... a goodsome armful for a warm and
zumly fire.

I wouldn't be surprised if **Granny** *didn't pronounce all her 'f's
as 'v's. And, not to put too fine a point on it ... all her 's's as
'z's!*

But cushla-cushla ... look at these tears ... rolling down your hazel-down cheeks like streams to a river!

Molly   They are nothing Granny. Just tears for the place of us poor peasantry in the very flattest plain of the landscape we call society ... and God's poor animal kind below that even! While up on the green hills folk who would call themselves *gentle* hurl sticks and stones of privilege and scorn!

Granny   Cushla-cushla, lambkin-mine, I cannot see through the thickets and hedges of these fancy book-learning words for the speckled eggs of truth in your chest nest!

Molly   I'm sorry, Granny. It's all my schooling which my rich aunt spent all those golden sovereigns upon. I declare, I've quite lost the clear, easy, country way of speaking like you!

Granny   Ah, upson-downson, my darling bud of May ... why don't you ramble down to the brook and wash your eyes clear ...

Molly   I will.

Granny   ... and then tell Granny-goodie all about it!

Molly *exits.*

Granny   It'll be something to do with men and field and lane mischief ... mark my words, zum lovesome lad has crept his harvest hand into my little haywain's cornstook!

Meanwhile ...

Betsy (*off*)   Oh Milady ... I've told that boot boy to be sure and a-rub down your boots first after old Sir Helstone ... otherwise he'll feel the sharp end of my tongue and no mistake! (*Enters.*) ... and now to take off all that fine attire ... Milady ... Milady? Where is she?

Meanwhile ...

Granny Now, I'll go out with these kindlins and faggots and break them up into firey-sticks to warm my baby lambkin!

She exits.

Meanwhile . . .

Betsy Ah . . . I spot Milady . . . pacing up and down, down and up before her long windows which overlook his Lordship's deer park! Pardon me, Mum, but would Milady like me to lug ten buckets of hot water up the four flights of stairs for a bath for you?

Harriet (*off*) What? . . . Who? . . . Where? . . . Oh. I was in a reverie! Who calls?

Betsy 'Twas I, Milady . . . Your pert Cheapside maid!

Harriet (*off*) Oh, Betsy . . . 'tis you!

Betsy 'Tis I! Would Milady like me to lug ten buckets of hot water up the four flights of stairs for a bath for you?

Harriet (*entering*) Why not?

Betsy Why not indeed . . . *Miladyship*? I'll go down to the well then, Milady . . .

Harriet Wait Betsy! I am in the humour for listening to your Cheapside wisdom!

Betsy Very well, Milady. On what matter, Milady?

Harriet On the matter of . . . love. Why love? Why do questions of love throb a threnody across the strings of my heart? It must be Lord Rothermere . . . or someone I've yet to meet . . . Betsy . . . have you ever been in love?

Betsy Love, Milday? *Me*, Milady? Why . . . Milady . . . what with Lord Rothermere, Lord Harry Squiffley, Sir Ranulph Dukes, even dear senile old Lord Helstone your dear father . . . catching me in every nook, cranny and window embrasure in the stately pile, saying 'Just be kind to this gentrified member, mi dear' . . . what with the stable staff liking to pounce on me from behind every stallion and mare . . . saying 'Look at this grass-snake I found . . . un's rearing up' . . . what with after I've retired from putting you to bed at two in the morning . . . I've got the boot boys, the gentlemen's gentlemen, even Mr Dunsey the butler a-forcing their way into my unlocked door and up my unbleached nightdress . . . saying 'How's about *this* for a warming-pan handle?' And then I've got to be up at six a-hot-ironing your fine dresses! No, no, no Milady . . . we servants are not gentle enough for love!

Harriet   I suppose not! Ah Betsy . . . it is so much harder for we gentry!

Betsy   Milady.

Harriet   I'll have my bath now.

Betsy   Milady.

She exits.

Harriet   Ah . . . where is love? They say love tames. They say love soothes the unquiet heart. They say love is a deer which stands in the forest glade and the lion, the tiger, the wolf kneel down before its gentleness and the air about the forest glade is green and clear. Why am I thinking of love? I'll stop. There . . . I've stopped. I'll have my supper and think of food. And then . . . I'll do . . . charitable works just as Mama wishes me to do . . . I'll take that poor peasant girl I met this afternoon some gift to show that I do have a heart! Yes . . . that's what I shall do!

She exits.

Meanwhile . . .

Molly   Oh, I am so refreshed by my dip in the brook! Yet not refreshed! Granny! Granny! Out breaking up

the firey-sticks I shouldn't wonder! I'll sit here and muse
till she returns and then I can pour out my heart to her
about that accursed Lady Helstone! Yes ... I shall muse
... On what? I'll muse ... on love. Why love? They
say love excites. They say love awakens the sleeping
heart. They say love is a tiger which walks in the forest
glade and the lamb, the deer, the goat put their heads
in its open mouth and the air in the forest glade is red
and hot. Why am I thinking about love? I'll stop. There
... I've stopped. I'll have my supper and think of food.
And then ... I'll make a corn dolly ... just as Granny
likes me to ... and I'll make one like that grand Milady
and throw her on the fire ... Yes ... that's what I shall
do!

The First Broken-Hearted Woman Sings an Angry Song

Harriet *enters reading* Her Aching Heart.

Harriet (*reading*) 'I'll make a corn dolly ... just as
Granny likes me to ... and I'll make one like that
grand Milady and throw her on the fire ... Yes ...
that's what I shall do!' ...

She laughs.

Yeah ... go for it! Burn that grand Milady!

She sighs. She sings ...

Song: Good Manners

   Sally came from the North
   She met Jane on a train
   They clicked right away
   They'd got plenty to say
   They conversed without any strain
   They had

Good manners
Good manners
That's what you need
  nice couple
  fun twosome

Soon, hey, they were doing it
Got in, switched out the light
And with no screaming
Eyes closed as if dreaming
And they did it only at night
They had
Good manners
Good manners
That's what you need
  nice couple
  fun twosome

Well Jane gets bored with this scene
She starts dating Louise
They're both on the floor
Sally walks through the door
She'd have knocked but Jane gave her the keys
She had
Good manners
Good manners
That's what you need
  nice couple
  fun threesome

Jane says 'This is Louise
She just lives down the street'
Sally gets a knife
And ends Louise's life
With a wound in her heart, she's so neat
She had
Good manners
Good manners
That's what you need

nice ending
fun funeral . . .

She stops singing.

Oh . . . Fuck It!!!

She reads the book again.

'There . . . that's the corn dolly finished at last . . . now
to throw it on the fire . . .'

She exits reading.

Chapter Five: High and Low

Molly *has been making a corn dolly during the last song.*

Molly   There . . . that's the corn dolly finished at last
. . . now to throw it on the fire . . . (*She looks at it.*) But
it's so beautiful . . . so perfect . . . so . . . this is the finest
corn dolly I've ever made . . . it looks like . . . it looks
like . . . (*Guess who it looks like.*)

*There is a sound of the thundering hooves belonging to six horses
pulling a racing perch-phaeton.*

What's that? A carriage passing by so late at night?
What ho . . . it's stopping close by. (*It is . . .*) It must be
some of the young rakes from Helstone Hall coming to
watch a cock fight in the back room of 'The Jolly
Wreckers' . . . our local hostelry . . .

She returns to her corn dolly. Off, we hear an exchange of voices.

Harriet (*off*)   Sirrah, lowly old crone . . . Direct me to
the humble cottage of the young maid with the flaxen
hair who this day disrupted the Helstone Hunt!

Granny (*off*)   Why gentle lady, she mun live behind
the rose-grown wattle and daub of thiz very fragrant
herb bed! Her name be Molly Penhallow . . . And she

mun be my lovesome grandchilder!

Harriet (*off*)   Then bend your back so I may use you as a step to descend from this coach!

Molly (*who has been listening to this exchange*)   Why ... I declare ... the ankle of this corn dolly is not quite straight! (*She twists the corn dolly's ankle slightly.*)

Off we hear ...

Harriet (*off*)   Aaaaaaaaaagh!!!

Molly   There!

Harriet (*off*)   Damme ... I have turned my ankle on your rounded old back, crone!

Granny (*off*)   Lord love you fine lady ... I am old ... there was a time when I could take the full weight of many a fine gentleman and lady on my strong yeowoman's shoulders!

Harriet (*off*)   Silence! Hold my horses while I limp into yonder low cottage!

Granny (*off*)   Oh what fine beasts! Cushla-a-cushla you fine stallions!

Harriet   Is it this way? ... (*She limps in.*) Ah ... there you are.

Molly   Yes Madam.

Harriet   I have had naught but ill-luck since you cursed me so roundly in the thorn thicket! The bath my maid Betsy prepared scalded me ... At dinner I was seated next to deaf Lady Aurelia Dumbarton on the one side, burping, belching and farting Lord Sir Jingo Wakefield on t'other! I had no appetite for the soup à la reine removed with fillets of turbot, with an Italian sauce; the chickens à la tarragon flanked by a dish of spinach and croutons, the glazed ham, cold partridges, some broiled mushrooms and the braised mutton pie.

Even the baskets of pastries, the Rhenish cream, the
jelly, the Savoy cake, the dish of salsify fried in butter,
the omelette and the anchovy sauce failed to tempt me.
The champagne was flat. The burgundy heavy. Dunsey,
the oaf, dropped Rhenish cream on my blue and I had
to change into my white! I went down to the stables and
Thunderer had cast a spavin! And now I've turned my
ankle on that wretched crone's back!

Molly   What care I for all that? Save that the
wretched crone is my beloved grandmother.

Harriet   Thunder 'n' Turf!!! I'll throw her some
sovereigns when I leave!

Molly   Then throw them now. There is the door.

Harriet   I have brought you something.

Molly   I want nothing of you.

Harriet   This you will. 'Tis a young roe-deer from my
father's park. Its mother died in a ... cooking accident.
It must be suckled. All creatures of the park and forest
love you. (*Long pause.*) You will tend it and stroke it and
kiss its downy head. (*Long pause.*) You will let it suck milk
from your fingers and nibble at your palm. (*Long pause.*)

Molly   All creatures of the park and forest ...

Harriet   ... love you. Yes.

Molly   I will ...

Harriet   ... tend it and ...

Molly   ... stroke it and ...

Both   ... kiss its downy head.

Harriet   Yes.

Molly   I will let it ...

Harriet   ... suck ...

Molly   . . . milk from my fingers and . . .

Harriet   . . . nibble . . .

Molly   . . . at my . . .

Harriet   . . . palm. Palm.

Molly   Where is this . . . deer?

Harriet   In my . . . Perch-Phaeton.

She goes to get the deer.

Molly   Oh what is happening? What is happening? (*In her confusion, she twists the limbs of her corn dolly.*) I am all . . . awry! I am all at sea! Within I am storm-tossed!

Off, we hear . . .

Harriet (*off*)   Aagh . . . what is happening to me . . . My limbs are not my own . . . They are twisted this way and that way as if by some supernatural force!

Granny (*off*)   Lord love you, Milady . . . have a care! I cannot hold these horses if you mun dance around so in front of un!

Harriet (*off*)   Hold the horses fool! Oh, how sea-sick I feel! I'll take out the roe-deer while you . . . Oh, I am twisted again . . .

Granny (*off*)   Milady . . . if you fall upon me so with yon roe-deer in your arms I mun can't stay these frisky stallions!

There is the sound of hooves ploughing, horses neighing, a perch-phaeton being pulled back and forth over something soft. There is a heart-rending scream, reminiscent of a young animal in anguish. Then silence.

Granny (*off*)   Oh . . . Milady!!

Harriet *enters with a limp-looking roe-deer in her arms.*

Harriet   I do naught around you but cover myself in

the blood of forest creatures.

Molly   Give the deer to me.

She takes it.

Molly   Ah ... it's still warm. I'll lay it here ... before the glowing fire. Stand back Madam ... you have done enough this night!

Harriet *stands back.*

Harriet   How firm she is!

Molly   Let me observe this soft body ...

Harriet   How softly she looks ...

Molly   Let me feel this tiny ... *beating*! ... heart ...

Harriet   How the firelight warms her red cheeks ...

Harriet *might be taking snuff at this time.*

Molly   If I gently rub here ... on this creature's breast ...

Harriet   Oh ... her hands!

Molly   And try to breathe some life into its tender mouth ...

Harriet   She kisses ...

Molly   Oh, she breathes ... her breast swelled and she took in air ... and, oh look ... not dead ... but merely in a swoon!

The deer perks up.

The following speeches together ... as **Harriet** *crouches by the deer and she and* **Molly** *excitedly seize each other's hands.*

Molly   Oh look ... the dear, dear thing ... its large eyes look up so trustingly ... its gentle soul stares into mine ... its breast heaves with life ... oh I am overcome!

Harriet   Oh look . . . the dear, dear thing . . . its large eyes look up so trustingly . . . its gentle soul stares into mine . . . its breast heaves with life . . . oh I am overcome!

Harriet *is not referring to the deer. They are holding hands.*

Molly   I am so glad it is alive!

Harriet   What is alive?

Molly   The deer . . .

Harriet   Oh the deer. Yes.

Molly   Milady . . . you hold my hands . . .

Harriet   Oh . . . so I do!

Molly   Loose them . . . if you will.

Harriet   Of course. (*She does.*) Tralala!

Molly   And take your deer back to your father's deer park.

Harriet   But I brought him for . . .

Molly   I cannot accept him. I hate you from the bottom of my heart. Please go.

Harriet   Look into my eyes and say that . . .

Molly   Please go.

Harriet   The part about hate . . .

Molly (*looks into her eyes*)   I . . . (*Long pause.*)

Harriet   Yes . . . ?

Molly   . . . hate . . . you . . . from the . . . bottom of my heart.

Harriet *seizes* **Molly** *by the arms.*

Harriet   Listen to me, peasant!!! I will not have it!
Will not have this hate for me! I will turn it into
something else though what I know not! And mark this
. . . Madam . . . I am the wilful, spoilt impetuous Lady
Harriet Helstone of Helstone Hall and I always . . .
always Get Whatso'er I Want!!!

Molly   And mark this . . . Lady Harriet Helstone . . .
(*As she says this she flings off* **Harriet***'s hands and stands tall.*)
I am Molly Penhallow of Penhallow Hollows . . . and I
never . . . *never* . . . Give In To Anyone!!! Here . . . (*She
thrusts the deer into* **Harriet***'s arms.*) Now go!

Harriet   I will! But I shall return!

Molly   You will not. You shall not return!

The deer follows this exchange.

Harriet   Madam . . . you have met your match!

Molly   And you Madam . . . have met yours!

Harriet *exits.* **Molly***, in fury, picks up the corn dolly . . . she
hurls it to the floor.*

Off we hear . . .

Harriet (*off*)   Open that Perch-Phaeton door!
Bend your back, woman . . .
Aaagh . . . I am hurled to the floor!
Catch the deer . . . catch i . . .

*There is a ploughing of hooves, frightened whinnying and a
horrifying crunch . . . as of a young roe-deer being run over by a
perch-phaeton wheel. Silence. Then . . .*

Granny   Oh. Lord love you . . . lackaday . . . see how
that poor little deer a-flew through the air and landed
upson-downson right under your carriage wheels
Milady!!

Harriet   Out of my way . . . peasant!!!

The carriage drives off.

The Second Broken-Hearted Woman Sings a Restless Song

As the carriage drives off, **Molly,** *furious, struggles out of her clothes. Underneath she is wearing a T-shirt and tracksuit. She sings.*

Song: Restless

Molly
It's hot, it's late, it's dark
Hey wasn't that the door?
I thought I heard something
I thought I saw . . .
Jumpy . . .
Restless . . .
A cat? A dog? A shape?
That creaking floor
I thought I heard something
I thought I saw

There's a face at the window
There's a hand on the door

It's here, it's there, it's gone
I don't believe in ghosts
I thought I heard something
I thought I saw . . .
Jumpy
Restless
It's white, it's grey, it's there
I don't believe in them
I thought I heard something
I thought I saw . . .

There's someone out there somewhere
With a hand on the door . . .

Fuck it . . . Oh fuck it! (*She picks up* Her Aching Heart, *reads.*) 'The Perch-Phaeton bearing the Lady Harriet sped through the dark night . . . in the corner . . . on the plush seat . . . Harriet leaned back discontentedly against the squabs . . .

Harriet *enters, wearing an old towelling dressing gown. She is reading* Her Aching Heart.

Harriet   '. . . Molly sat in the now-dying embers of the cottage fire . . . the rush candles barely lit the simple room . . .'

As she reads . . . **Molly** *picks up the phone and dials.*

Harriet   '. . . Molly's mind was a turmoil of emotions . . . of heartbreak for the fox, of yearning for the baby roe-deer . . . but most of all . . . there was burning hatred for Lady Harriet Helstone . . .'

Harriet's *telephone rings. She picks it up.*

Hello?

Molly   Hello . . . hi . . . it's Molly . . . we met at the LGCIF confer . . .

Harriet   Oh yes, hello, how are you?

Molly   Oh . . . you know . . .

Harriet   Oh yes.

Molly   So. What you up to?

Harriet   Oh me. Well . . . I'm *reading.*

Molly   Oh no! Me too! What you reading?

Harriet   It's called *Her Aching Heart.*

Molly   Oh no! Me Too!!!

Harriet   No????

Molly   Yes!!!! Isn't that weird??? Where you up to?

Harriet (*reads*)   'The Perch-Phaeton bearing the Lady Harriet sped through the dark night . . .' She's just totalled the deer . . . where are you up to?

Molly (*reads*)   'Molly's heart was a turmoil of emotions . . .'

Harriet   I wonder why?

Molly   She's feeling hatred for Lady Harriet . . .

Harriet   Oh, sure!

Molly   So, do you think they're in love?

Harriet   No!!!!!!

Molly   Poor fuckers!

Harriet   Yes!

Molly   So, listen, anyway . . . are you doing anything Thursday?

Harriet   No . . . no, I'm not.

Molly   So . . . do you fancy doing anything?

Harriet   Me? Oh . . .

Molly   Well . . . we could do something nice.

Harriet   That would be nice.

Molly   So I'll think of something, shall I . . . and ring you . . . Wednesday . . .

Harriet   Okay. That'd be nice.

There is a pause.

Molly   Well . . . back to your book . . .

Harriet   Back to yours.

Molly   Good night.

Harriet   Good night.

Two Women With Hearts on the Mend Sing a Song

Song: It's Spring -- Hearts Mend

Crawling out from under a stone
An egg-white termite blinks at the light
A slug tracks across a leaf
Its shiny trail shines in the weak sun
Black dots before my eyes in the garden
I'm not dizzy, they're early gnats
The surface of the pond is bubbling and frothing
Frogs clinging together
Tadpole jelly on its way

It's spring
Heart mend
Why not sing?

Hung like millions of mighty hammocks
Cobwebs in the corners of all my rooms
Blowing like tumbleweed in Kansas
The fluff under my bed's a disgrace
Like the plimsoll line on a ship
The black tidemark on my bath must go
Like what leaked from the *Torrey Canyon*
The grease on my cooker could kill a seal
Spring-cleaning is on its way

It's spring
Hearts mend
Why not sing?

Eating less Kit-Kat's and Cheesy Quavers
Losing a couple of pounds
Walking to work every single morning
Going to Dancercise every week
Buying the *Guardian* not the *Mirror*
Reading only improving books
To the launderette before the pile's gigantic
Never wearing knickers twice.

New beginning is on its way

It's spring
Hearts mend
Why not sing?

The song builds to a stirring crescendo.

Act Two

Chapter Six: A Fop

A fop's room. **Lord Rothermere** *enters with many starched neckerchiefs. He is trying to tie one round his neck. Although in these penurious times he may bear a passing resemblance to* **Molly** *in a curly black wig he is a* completely different person.

Rothermere M'name's Rothermere . . . Peer of the Realm! and I'm trying to tie m'damn neckerchief! (*He spoils one.*) Damme! (*Hurls it to the floor, takes another.*) I'm trying to achieve *The Waterfall* . . . But the damn thing looks more like the Ruddy *Rain Butt*. Haw Haw Haw! M'rusticating here with the Helstones because m'pockets are to let! Mortgaged m'family seat on a curricle race and I lorst. Haw Haw Haw! So I'm down here courting the Lady Harriet . . . trying to cut a dash! (*He spoils another one. Hurls it to the floor.*) Damme! (*Takes another.*) She's a damn shrew . . . but she's good bloodstock and she's worth twenty thousand a year so m'pressing m'suit! She's no plain Jane so I don't mind mounting the filly and riding her hard to the bridle and curbing her to rein if you get m'meaning! Zounds . . . think I've done it! (*He lowers his chin carefully over the Waterfall.*) Splendid! Splendid!!!! Thing is . . . this hellcat's rather hard to bring about to the *bit* of late . . . Winces when I steal a buss . . . Snarls when I put m'hand to her bodice . . . No matter . . . L'offer for her . . . bed her . . . get her breeding . . . the friskiest mare trots to harness once she's in foal! (*He has been putting on his coat, his quizzing glass.*) I'll take the whip to her this very eve after supper!

He exits.

Chapter Seven: A Yokel

A yokel enters with a bunch of simple hedgerow flowers. Although in these penurious times he may bear a passing resemblance to **Harriet** *in a red wig he is a* completely different *character.*

Joshua   Oi'm Joshua, good gentlefolk and ladies! Oi'm stable laad up at Helstone Hall . . . and Oi'm a-taking these hedgerow blooms to Penhallow Hollows cos I'm a-courtin!!! Farther said 'Are ee after old Granny Penhallow then?' and I roars and says '*No* father . . . her's too *oldsome*! Oi'm arfter Miss Molly!' And ee, Farther, says, 'You go careful now young laad, they Penhallows look red as roses but they got briars as I know when Oi troied to tumble Miss Molly's Maa . . . she put up a devil of a foight till I tied er with some hedging twine . . . ere . . . I ope when I caught 'er t'weren't about nine months afore Molly were dropped on straw . . . else an' she's yore sister!!!' And I said 'Oi don't care an' she's my sister, Farther, for that would make us close and anyway what do it matter, you'm tied every woman in this village with yore hedging twine so any lass moight be moi sister!' Oi love Miss Molly sore. Her's all the world to me.

Meanwhile, in the present day, the phone rings. **Harriet** *goes to answer it.*

Harriet   Hello? Hi . . . hello! I'm fine. How are you? Yeah . . . I did get to work on time . . . just! Yes . . . it was nice. Yes . . . me too. I was going to ring you tonight . . . see if you fancied . . . You don't know what I was going to say! Yes . . . that was what I was going to say! Yes . . . you come to me this time . . . it's only fair! (*She smiles.*) Yes . . . that would be fine . . . perfect. About then then. 'Bye. 'Bye. (*She puts down the phone.*)

Meanwhile, **Molly Penhallow** *enters with something cupped in her hands.*

Joshua (*covered with confusion*)   Oh, Fence and Stoyle . . .

here comes Miss Molly now!

Molly   Oh Joshua . . . I was conversing with this
fledgling which lives in the old oak tree in the lane . . .
and it leaned so far over the nest side to hear my
murmurings that it did fall out onto the lane and I fear
it is in a swoon!

Joshua   Oh Miss Molly . . . how all woild creatures do
love ee . . . put it down on the ground here . . . I will
help ee make all better.

Molly   Oh Joshua . . . how kind you are . . . how full
of gentleness!

She lays the fledgling down on the ground before **Joshua**. *He
lifts up his foot and stamps on it.*

Joshua   There . . . Miss Molly . . . that's put the little
thing out of its misery! Here . . . Oi brought you these
hedgerow blossoms . . . they are for . . . besoide yore
bed.

Molly *takes the hedgerow blossoms.*

Molly   Joshua . . . Take that. (*She brings down the bunch
on his head.*) And that . . . (*She knees him in the groin.*) And
that . . . (*She punches him on the chin.*)

Joshua   Miss Molly . . .

Molly   Is all the world mad??? Cannot all things *live*???
Cannot all things *be*??? A bird . . . a deer . . . a fox . . .
all dead? Ah . . . everything swims in blood!!!!

She runs off.

Joshua   A bird . . . (*He sees the bird, what's left of it.*)
A deer? . . . a deer????
A fox? . . . a fox????
I don't remember stamping on no deers and foxes!
She mun be in a fever of some sort.
Oh lord . . . her's put oi in a daze . . .
Which way am I walking . . . ?

He exits.

As **Joshua** *wanders dazedly off, the present-day* **Molly** *returns engrossed in* Her Aching Heart.

Molly (*reads*)   '. . . the gentle giant was in a daze. Why had she served him thus? Why had she dealt him those unjust blows? He was a simple man . . . honest, true, with no deceit . . . he saw, but could not comprehend, her anguish. He knew it could not be for the bird, though for the bird . . . and the creatures of the wild wood it seemed to be . . . he shrugged and followed her down the lane . . .'

During this read account . . . **Joshua** *might make some confused sounds offstage to show his confusion.*

'As the sad youth strolled despondently away . . . in the arbour of the darkly-forbidding, ivy-covered Helstone Hall . . . standing under the leafy canopy of oak, beech, elm, silver birch, laburnum, sycamore, ash, willow, hawthorn, Douglas fir, Norway spruce, Austrian pine . . .' Oh come on . . . enough with the trees! '. . . the discontented Lady Harriet sighed at the waxing moon . . .'

She exits.

Chapter Eight: A Misfortune

Lady Harriet *enters.*

Harriet   Ah . . . me . . . (*Sighs.*) Lackaday! (*Sighs.*) Oh moon . . . when you look down on me with your pale silvery face cover'd o'er with dark-scudding clouds . . . what do you see? You see yourself in me! I am become you . . . a pale planet that circumnavigates this globe, the earth look you, not there, not there at all when the sun shines . . . and then, at night I rise . . . clamber

slowly behind the clouds up, up into the star-tossed sky
... to hang like a pearl upon a maiden's breast ...
rising and falling with her ululating breath ... oh ... I
am become quite moonsick! What do I seek? To
conquer ... yes. To invade ... oh yes. To colonise ...
oh yes yes yes! But to conquer ... invade ... colonise
... what? What do I seek? Where do I seek? Who do I
seek?

During the last eight lines, **Lord Rothermere** *has appeared
and listens to her mooning.*

Rothermere   Strap me ... the filly's in heat! Now to
get m'feet in her stirrups ... m'thighs gripped tight
around her steaming shanks and ride ride ride! (*He steals
up behind her, puts his hands on her breasts.*) What ho, Lady
Harriet!

Harriet   AAAgh! (*Looks down at the hands.*) Oh ... what
ho, Lord Rothermere. Take your bejewelled hands off
m'fichu.

Rothermere   Or what, Madam?

Harriet   Or I will bend back the finger on which rests
the Rothermere Ruby and it will snap like a chicken leg.

He takes away his hands.

I am not in the humour for social intercourse, My Lord.

Rothermere   'Twas not *social* intercourse I had in
mind, My Lady.

Harriet   What then?

Rothermere   I have this hour had private word with
your father in the library, sweet lady. Because of my fine
lineage, my owning of two counties ... and the relative
lack of madness in m'family ... he has encouraged me
to press m'suit and offer you m'hand, m'heart ... and
any other of m'manly parts in marriage!

Harriet   Marriage?

Rothermere   Ay . . . marriage . . . and all that goes
with the mingling together of bloodlines!

Harriet   I do not wish to marry, Sir.

Rothermere   Come come, m'dear . . . you are not in
your first bloom of youth . . . good men are hard to
find.

Harriet   'Tis true.

Rothermere   Your father says I am to insist . . . Lady
. . . I have the starting price . . . now race with me!

Harriet   I will not, Sir!

Rothermere   Madam, you will!

He lunges for her, she throws him off.

Harriet   No!

Rothermere   Yes!

He lunges again. She throws him off.

Rothermere   Yes!

Harriet   No!
Sir . . . if you snatch at me again . . .
I shall have no recourse but to defend myself . . .

Rothermere   With what my lady?
The arbour is secluded . . . and the house guests all
playing billiards!

Harriet   With . . . with . . . oh . . . with this sword so
fortuitously discarded earlier today by my brother Harry!

She picks up the fortuitously discarded sword.

Rothermere   Cross swords with me, would you,
Milady? Very well! (*He draws his sword, which luckily he had
decided to wear to supper that evening.*) I will fence thee into a

corner, into a sweat, into a swoon and then into a bed!
En garde!

Harriet   *En garde!*

They fence. Obviously if they can cut candles in two, swing from chandeliers, do stunts etc. . . . this would be favourite.

Rothermere *nicks* **Harriet** *on the arm.*

Rothermere   Ah . . . first blood!
I will draw other blood from ye yet, lady!

Harriet *(recovering bravely)*   That ye will not, fight on!

They fight on. **Harriet** *lands a fatal body thrust.*

Rothermere   What? Who? How?
You have slain me!
So ends the line of Rothermere . . .
So empties that fine stable . . .
Off canters the last . . . stallion . . .

He dies.

Harriet   No . . . do not die! Curse you . . . you sack of malmsy . . . live!! Live!!!! He's dead! Damme damme damme!!! What can I do? I'll hide him . . . here . . . under this . . . *(She checks.)* Betula pendula . . . *(She drags him off.)* Oh, how my wound pains me! But it is as naught compared with the agony in my heart . . . what am I to do? The house is full of Rothermere's cronies . . . See them, by the light of many candles, a-playing billiards . . . if they knew what I have just done . . . they would lay me on that green field of baize . . . and with their great cues shoot their balls into my body's pockets . . . such is our class's notion of after-supper sport! Who to turn to? . . . My father . . . I have killed a suitor! . . . My mother . . . was dallying with Rothermere . . . Oh, what an ill-starred woman I am! Breathless, Friendless and Helpless. It is all the fault of that pretty peasant! All from her curse! She shall learn humility . . . desperation

and agonising pain. I shall go to her cottage and . . .
and kill her too!!!!

She exits.

Chapter Ten: A Lowly Bed

Molly *enters. She is wearing a cloak.*

Molly   What a strange, wild night it is! I have been
out wandering amid the sights and sounds and smells of
the darkness . . . such sights I have seen . . . such sounds
I have heard . . . such smells I have . . . I found myself
in my restless roaming close by Helstone Hall . . . what
took me there I know not . . . and as I stared up at the
first-floor windows . . . where . . . where the ladies of the
house do sleep . . . I heard a piteous moaning in the
undergrowth . . . and there lay a man . . . sore run
through with a sword . . . he was at death's door . . .

There is a knocking.

Who's that at the door?

There is a creaking as of a door opening.

Granny? Back from her midnight rites up at the
standing stones? Aaagh?

Lady Harriet *enters, cloaked, with sword in hand.*

Harriet   So! So my fine curser! So my ill-fortune-teller!
So my unlucky star! So . . . Oh!!!

She swoons in a dead faint in **Molly***'s arms.*

Molly   Oh . . . you have fainted! (*She carries her to the
bed.*) Oh . . . you are so hot! (*She takes off her cloak.*) Oh
. . . you are hurt! (*Touches the wound.*) But not badly!

*She bathes her forehead, binds her arm, puts a cover over her, looks
down at her.*

A Woman with a Mended Heart Realises Something

Molly   Fuck it.
Oh fuck it!

She sings . . .

Song: In Love Again

> I am not myself again
> Anxious, scared, on edge again
> Wondering who she's with again
> Wondering where she is again
> All the time in a spin again
> Hours together so short again
> Heart leaps when she's at the door again
> Curled together on the floor again
> The bed not my own again
> Waiting for the phone again
> Heart like a hand-grenade
> Heart like a bunch of flowers
> Like a just-hatched bird again
> Like a recent wound again
> Like a soft-boiled egg again
> Like a purple bruise again
> Taking taxis across town again
> Damn damn damn damn
> In love again

Molly   (*sighs, then lies down beside* **Harriet**, *turns away from her on her side*)   Fuck it!

Harriet   (*wakes with a start, sees where she is, sees* **Molly**)
Fuck it. Oh fuck it!

She sings . . .

> I am in the soup again
> Sky is blue, then dark again
> Fairground's come to town again
> Circus with its acts again

All the time in a stew again
Grand Opera seems quite small
Fear strikes, it's the *News at Ten*
Was she there, where is she then?
My peace of mind is gone again
Words tell lies in poems again
Heart like a forest fire
Heart like a sparkling sea
Like a trampoline again
Like a traffic jam again
Like a field of flowers again
Like an upturned car again
Playing Radio Two all day again
Damn damn damn
In love again

(*Lies down away from* **Molly**.) Fuck it.

They sleep, or so it seems. They are turned away from one another. With a sleepy sigh they both turn on their backs. They lie there. With a sleepy sigh, **Harriet** *turns to* **Molly**. *They lie there. With a sleepy sigh,* **Molly** *turns to* **Harriet**. *They lie there. They both have a disturbing dream, or so it seems. The disturbing dream makes them toss and murmur and throw themselves into each other's arms.*

Harriet   What? . . .

Molly   No . . .

Harriet   How? . . .

Molly   Plea . . .

Harriet   Here . . .

Molly   Now . . .

Harriet   Yes . . .

Molly   Yes . . .

They lie there. They pull each other closer and closer. They begin to roll from one side to another. They swap places. They lie there.

*They let each other go. They turn onto their backs. They lie there
. . . Then . . . they murmur and roll back. They toss and turn and
roll back into their original positions. They turn away from each
other. They lie there.* **Harriet** *opens her eyes.*

Harriet   Where am I?

Molly   You are in a lowly bed in Penhallow Hollows,
Milady.

Harriet   What am I doing there?

Molly   You were sore wounded, Madam . . . and you
came . . . to kill me, I think.

Harriet   Ah yes, now I remember. (*Pause.*) I have had
the strangest dream.

Molly   Oh . . . Milady?

Harriet   I dreamed that I was in this bed awake . . .
and I was lost . . . and I reached out . . . and I took a
precious body . . . like mine own . . . into my arms . . .
and pulled her close . . . and . . . held this precious body
to my heart . . . as though she were mine own. And
then I woke and it was all a dream.

Pause.

Molly   I too had the strangest dream.

Harriet   Oh . . . Madam?

Molly   I dreamed that I was in this bed awake . . . and
I was scared . . . and I reached out . . . and I took a
precious soul . . . like mine own . . . into my arms . . .
and pulled it close . . . and drew this precious soul into
my heart . . . as though she were mine own. (*Pause.*) And
then I woke up and it was all a dream.

Pause.

Harriet   It seems we have the same dream.

Molly   It seems we do.

They turn to face one another.

Harriet Mine was no dream.

Molly Nor mine.

Harriet I was awake.

Molly I too.

Harriet What can it mean?

Molly I think it means we must kiss.

Harriet I think it must mean that too.

They kiss.

Molly I have not read of this thing in any of my wide reading!

Harriet Nor I.

They kiss again.

Harriet Your kiss lights up the sky with fiery rays. It fills my ears with birdsong.

Molly No . . . it's the dawn . . . the day races on apace . . . what brought you to my bed last night? My heart fears for you . . . Your poor arm . . . how?

Harriet Last eve . . . I did kill a man!

Molly Oh! (*She clutches her breast.*)

Harriet He would have wedded, bedded and blood-shedded me . . .

Molly Oh!

Harriet So I slew him in fair fight! I hid his lifeless body under a Betula pendula close by my father's house.

Molly Oh!

Harriet But mark this . . . my angel (*She swiftly kisses* **Molly**.) . . . no eyes saw our postes and ripostes . . . no

ears heard our panting, thus can I tell this tale which I
have devised ... I will return to the house saying that
while Rothermere and I walked in the arbour ... a
savage band of smugglers fell upon us ... Rothermere
defended me with his life ... but there were too many
of them and he was sadly overcome ... and run
through by the leader ... a man full seven feet high ...
these blackguards then did bind me and take me as
hostage ... I was hurled to the belly of their boat ...
but they, being of the lower orders ... knew not how to
tie a rope ... and I unloosed myself, slid over the side
... and swam to shore ... which I reached as the dawn
rose!

Molly Oh!

This 'oh' has a different ring to it.

Harriet What think you of my tale?

Molly You say you killed this ... Rothermere?

Harriet Aye.

Molly And you hid him under a ...

Harriet Betula pendula, aye.

Molly Betula pendula ... is that a gentrified ...
Latinate name for ... spreading birch?

Harriet Aye ... what of it?

Molly I have a tale too, tho' not devised. Last eve ...
I wandered through the night air ... and found myself
beneath your windows ...

Harriet My dove!

Molly I stood in the trees, fearing apprehension ...
and there did stumble on the still form of a man ...
under a spreading birch ... He seemed at first dead ...
but I did kneel down and feeling a faint breath from his
rank mouth ... and a faint stirring from his manly chest

. . . I did breathe life into him . . . just as I did the roe-deer.

Harriet   He lives?

Molly   He lives! I hurled a stone at the window close by and gentlefolk came out and succoured him.

Harriet   You revived him?

Molly   Aye.

Harriet (*in a furious rage*)   You stupid bloody PEASANT!!! Why couldn't you keep your villagey snout out of the business of your high-born betters?

Molly (*starting to get into a furious rage*)   I beg your pardon, Madam! I had no notion when I performed my Christian deed on the poor man that you were in the habit of slaying every swain who lays a hand on you! We *villagey* maidens are more gentle!

Harriet   You villagey maidens are more meddlesome! I now, through your interfering, face the wrath of my parents, the contempt of society . . . and a possible stretch in Newgate!!!!

Molly   I thought only to save the poor man whom you no doubt *led* on in wilful high-bred fashion!

Harriet   I did not kneel down and *kiss* him with my open mouth, Madam!!!!

Molly   How *Dare* You????

Harriet   I *Dare* Anything, Madam!!! I must now, from your necrophiliac necking . . . hatch some New Plot to Escape from these surroundings!!

Molly   Hatch Away!!! Sit on your Big Bottom and Lay Your Foul Eggs, You Hen!!!

Harriet   *Hen?????*
Big Bottom????
Yeeeaghhhh!!!

Molly Grrrrrraghhhhh!

Harriet I will to the local hostelry ... There I will turn my eyes to some oafish swain ... I will lure him out to the barn and there, while we are dallying ... I will hit his head with a wattle and daub brick, seized from this very cote ...

Molly Those are my Granny's wattle and daub bricks, thief!

Harriet What Care I?
I will also, as *thief*, steal the oafish swain's clothes, brogues and purse. I will then to the harbour ... whence I will stow away on a boat to France. I will rid me of this devilish country and of this devilish maiden!

Molly Go then!

Harriet I go!

Molly Farewell forever!!!

Harriet Forever, farewell!!!

They stand staring at each other for a long time. **Harriet** *exits.*

A Woman In Love Tells the World's Funniest Joke

Song: The World's Funniest Joke

Molly
On the seventh day God said
'Well, that's everything
Except I haven't had a laugh all week'
And he started chuckling ...
'I'll create sex,' he said
'And I'll create love'

'And I'll stick them both together
And watch from up above ...'

It's a suit that won't fit
It's a hat that's too small
It's a pair of big baggy pants
It's the world's funniest joke

It's a comic monologue
It's a sitcom dialogue
It's a punchline in the gut
It's the world's funniest joke

Hold your sides
For see
The laugh's on me

It's the skin of a banana
It's a red plastic nose
It's a custard pie in the face
It's the world's funniest joke

It's French without Saunders
It's Cannon without Ball
It's Morecambe and it's not wise
It's the world's funniest joke

God said 'I'm glad I thought of this
Amusement that I've found
To have between performing miracles
Besides
It makes the world go round
Love messes up the sex,' he said
'Sex messes up the love
And I'm a spiritual deity
Who guffaws from above'

Hold your sides
You see
The laugh's on me.

I am sore disappointed with this secular world ... The
men are naught. The women ... are naught. I will don
this habit that dear Sister Winifred, the Scripture teacher
at my school, left me in her will ... and ... (*She takes*

the habit, starts to put it on.) I will enter the safe walls of the monastery of Our Lady of The Hollows on the outskirts of our village. In the warm hearts of the nuns there . . . In the singing of hymns the chanting of prayers the telling of rosaries I will find my peace. (*She is dressed.*)

The telephone rings.

Hello?

Harriet *appears, dressed in* **Joshua**'s *clothes, a little away from her.*

Harriet   Hello, opérateur . . . je veux parler avec zero zero un, un, zero, un, sept huit trois, quatre quatre cinque . . .

Molly   Hello?

Harriet   Is that you?

Molly   Hello . . . I can hardly hear you . . .

Harriet   Hello . . . is that better?

Molly   Better. Where are you?

Harriet   In Lyons. I got here!

Molly   Yes. Have you used my camping stove yet?

Harriet   Yes! We made spaghetti on it last night!

Molly   Did We? How are 'WE'?

Harriet   All right. We're learning to be friends again.

Molly   Oh. Nice. (*She makes a face.*)
So . . . it's a nice holiday then?

Harriet   It's all right. I miss you.

Molly   What? The line's crackling . . .

Harriet   I miss you!!!

Molly   I miss you too!

Harriet   I love you!

Molly   What? You're very faint!

Harriet   I love you!

Molly   I can't hear you, can you hear me?

Harriet   Yes, I can hear you, can you hear me?

Molly   Hello? Hello? . . . Hello? (*She listens.*) Ah . . . Monsieur . . . Est-ce qu'il y a l'opérateur . . . Oh, forget it! N'importe monsieur . . . au revoir! (*She puts the phone down.*)

Harriet   Hello? Hello? Hello? Fuck it! (*She puts the phone down.*)

Molly *exits for the convent.*

Chapter Eleven: Foreign Soil

Harriet   Well, here I am in France! My plot worked like a . . . well not like a dream . . . more a nightmare . . . the clod I lured into the barn . . . whose clothes I now wear . . . had such a thick pate I swear I had to hit him not once, not twice, but thrice to lay him out! And he appeared not to be breathing after that! Lackaday, what care I? What care I for ought? I am here in this strange foreign country with a hole where once for a brief interlude, beat my heart. I will look to the bright side. I will find myself a job, spying for the French . . . for Old Bonaparte will surely pay me well . . . intimate as I am with all the society, army and navy bigwigs! Now to hie me to a French spying headquarters . . . and take the King's shilling . . . le franc du roi . . . le franc du Napoleon . . . oh Heavens!!

She exits.

Chapter Twelve: Our Lady of The Hollows

Molly *comes in and kneels to prayer.*

Molly   Ah well, Lord, here I am, on my knees again! I
have now been in these your safe walls some forty days
. . . and forty long, long, achingly long nights. The first
ten days were filled with my urgent prayers for my dear
old friend Joshua . . . whose lifeless form I came across
in a barn as I made my wearisome way hither . . .
someone had savagely beaten him about the head with a
strangely familiar wattle and daub brick . . . and worse
still . . . made sport of him by dressing him in maid's
attire!!! I pray forgiveness and mercy and a taste of their
own medicine for the perpetrator of this dire deed!
Luckily I chanced to feel a breath of air from his kind
mouth . . . so I did put my lips to his and breathed life
into him. He lives . . . but I fear will never know the joy
of book-reading . . . For the rest . . . Lord . . . I
endeavour with your help to banish thoughts of . . . of
the secular world. I am wearing the hair-shirt under my
habit and it does take my mind off it a morsel.
Yours faithfully,
Sister Penhallow of The Hollows.

Chapter Thirteen: An Untimely Revolution

Harriet *enters, dressed as a tricoteuse . . . with revolutionary
bonnet and large piece of knitting. On her feet she wears sabots.*

Harriet   What a lucky stroke! As I was about to enter
the French spying headquarters I chanced to overhear
two Frenchies talking about some revolution that had
occurred and it seems that we aristocrats are cursed
unpopular . . . so I adopted a rough accent . . .
exchanged my men's attire for low foreign female tatters
and here I am in the square awaiting some public event
I know not what! My mind keeps wandering to England

... to Cornwall ... to Helstone village ... to that small lowly cote ... (*She starts knitting to take her mind off England.*) The women of the town told me to take up this dire occupation ... It keeps the hands busy but not the mind ... and not the heart ... what's that commotion over there? ... A cart full of finely-featured aristocratic gentlefolk rather like m'self ... they are taking them to that edifice ... with the sharp blade hovering at its top ... (*She knits and watches.*) They are bending them down under it ... with their necks resting on ... Oh my God!!! (*Tumbrils, cheering and the swish of a guillotine. More cheers.*) Oh horror ... get me out of here ... make way, lowly Frenchies ... way for a lady!!!

She exits.

Chapter Fourteen: A Nun in Torment

Molly *pacing up and down. She falls to her knees.*

Molly   Is this fair, God? Two ... three kisses ... and some almost ... *sisterly* embracing ... and for this I am in mortal agony!!! My body is on fire! Moisture courses from my eyes my armpits my ... everywhere! It is as if someone has hatched a nest of fledglings in my lap and they are treading my nest and crying out for worms!!! What is this torture???

Chapter Fifteen: An Aristocrat in Trouble

Meanwhile in France ... **Harriet** *chained up in a prison.*

Harriet   The chains chafe ... The floor is dank ... The cell is dark ... Jailers paws me. Rats gnaw me ... I am to be guillotined tomorrow. But all his is as *naught* compared to the strange unsettling disease I seem to have contracted! It is as if someone has hurled a bowl of hot soup into my loins ... and a mouse is swimming around inside it as if 'twere a bathing pool! It is such painful, exquisite torment ... It is such torture! I am in love with her! I cannot rest for thinking of her! I shouted and ran from her and now ... I am served with this most miserable anguish! Wait ... who's that at the door? It's a fop ... dressed all in scarlet ... and he carries a small flower ... why, it's a pimpernellus rubicus ... in common gardening lore ... A scarlet pimpernel!

She goes to explore. She exits.

Chapter Sixteen: Worse Torment

Molly   I am in love with her! I cannot rest for thinking of her! I called her 'Hen' and made mention of her Big Bottom ... and it's not so big!!!! ... and I drove her from me to her certain death! Oh Lord ... save her from danger! Bring her back to me ... And I will be your servant forever!

Chapter Seventeen: Two Nuns

As **Molly** *is praying* ... **Harriet** *enters dressed as a nun.*

Harriet   Oh how fortunate I am! The fop was no fop, but a brave and dauntless rescuer of Aristocrats caught short in The Frenchie Muddle! He brought me these religious weeds and I habited them and stole from the prison ... The Mighty Bastille! ... and with a posse of novice nuns as cover ... I took ship to this our mother convent! We arrived at dead of night ... so I know not where I am! I will discover what I can from this praying sister.

She kneels by **Molly**.

Harriet   Salvete, Sister!

Molly   Forgive me Sister . . . I know no Latin. (*She sighs.*) Save only . . . Betula pendula. (*She sighs again.*)

Harriet   Which simple folk call 'Spreading Birch'.

They look at each other.

Harriet   Molly.

Molly   Harriet.

Harriet   How?

Molly   Where?

Harriet   When?

Molly   Why?

Harriet   What care I?

Molly   And what care I?

Harriet   I love you.

Molly   I love you.

They kiss.

Harriet   Let us get out of this monastery . . . I have such a strange torment in me . . .

Molly   I also . . . But I cannot.

Harriet   Cannot?

Molly   I made a promise to God . . . that if He returned you safe to me I would devote myself to Him forever.

Harriet   You bloody stupid peasant!!!!

Molly   '. . . and she went back to London . . . and Molly stayed in the monastery all her livelong days . . . and they never saw each other again. The End.'

Harriet   That's how it finished?

Molly   Didn't you read it?

Harriet I left it behind in Lyons. It was driving me crazy . . . one of them in France . . . one of them in a fucking monastery!

Molly She was so miserable in that monastery.

Harriet She was fairly fucked off in France!

Molly Yes?

Harriet Yes.

Molly Hmm. You know when you phoned me from Lyons?

Harriet Yes?

Molly What did you want to tell me?

Harriet I love you.

Molly I love you too. Oooh . . .

Harriet What . . .

Molly My heart hurts . . .

Harriet Snap.

Both (*reprise of 'In Love Again'*)
    I am not myself again
    Ready, steady, go again
    Fairground's come to town again
    Circus with its acts again
    All time in a spin again
    Hours together so short
    Heart leaps, she's at the door again
    Curled together on the floor again
    The bed is not my own again
    I'll never sleep alone again
    Heart like a just-hatched bird
    Heart like a forest fire
    Like a bunch of flowers again
    Like a sparkling sea again
    Like a field of flowers again

Like a recent wound again
Oh, oh, my aching heart again
Hey, hey, hey hey
In love again
Ho ho, ho ho
In love again
Ha ha, ha ha
In love again
Oh oh, oh oh
In love again

Nothing Compares to You

Nothing Compares to You was first performed in March 1995 at the Birmingham Repertory Theatre, with the following cast:

Fylgia	Vicky Pepperdine
	Angela Clerkin
Mary	Sharon Muircroft
Lily	Lorna Laidlaw
Helen	Trisha Wilcox
Miriam/Rachel	Lou Wakefield
Joy	Karen Parker
John/Todd	Jamie Newall

Directed by Gwenda Hughes
Designed by Ruari Murchison

Fylgia (follower): in Norwegian folklore a guardian spirit, or one's double or soul. The fylgia often appears in dream-form in animal shape. If one sees a fylgia while awake it indicates death. When someone dies, the fylgia passes on to another member of the family.

Act One

This is a place of great beauty and detritus. There are perches and vantage points, possibly trapezes and ropes and facilities for flying and swooping and soaring in and out of modern, rather cramped, sad rooms, roadways and locations in various parts of Great Britain.

One: Snowy Landscape

Sinead O'Connor is heard singing 'Nothing Compares To U'.

*A **Fylgia** is revealed. Sound of a cold cold wind. The **Fylgia** shivers. It shivers a lot. Torn-up paper, like snow, falls specifically on the **Fylgia**. It sighs. Another **Fylgia** comes on pulling a sledge, on skis. It takes from the sledge a very very very long scarf which it winds round and round and round the first **Fylgia**. It takes a saw from the sledge and saws a circle in the stage. Fishes down it. Catches fish after fish. Lets the cold **Fylgia** fish. It fishes up an old tyre. A scream rings out. A dreadful sound of screeching tyres. Metal grinding against itself. **Fylgias** exit to assist in the next scene . . .*

Two: Arriving

Mary *is dying in a motorway accident. The bonnet of the car is pushed at such speed, it penetrates her chest, slicing her in two. She moves here from incredible pain, out of her body, into death. She is nowhere. She wears one glove. It is all very sudden. The* **Fylgias** *assist tenderly.*

Mary   OOOOOoooooooooooooooooooooooooooooooooooh!
OOooOOOh!
This is how it . . . ooooh . . . Is!
This is . . . Now. Now. Goodness.
It's not . . . it is . . . is . . . is . . . is

OOOooooh.
Extraordinary . . . it doesn't . . .
Ex . . . tra . . . ord . . . right through to . . .
I've peed.
Shit mys . . . shit.
OOoooooooooooh.
Incredible . . . it's . . . it . . . oh. Oh Oh.
Ten words for this . . . incredible inconceivable
insupportable intense inexorable in pain in shit in the
soup in pain . . .
No pain . . . Oh . . . No.
No anything. One glove.
No . . . None . . . Not . . . Oh.
It's . . .
oh oh oh oh it's cool ice hot warm nothing
hello anybody there here help me help oh
oh oh oh my mother Dad no no no
Yes I can . . . speak . . . Mary . . . it's Mary . . . yes . . .
esss . . . I can hear you . . . thank you!
Count!
How did I how did fish cod air
car car car car car
hurt no no hello hello help oh
Count! fish sex ice hot
tadpole tadpole????
motorway . . . ambulance . . . get the get the like a
helicopt . . . tailback tailback Junction . . . what what
what Fourteen . . . whup whup whup police-car roof!
no . . . no no . . . no no . . . no
high . . . going away . . . up up up . . . uppabove upppa
. . . oh oh oh . . .
high . . . high . . . high . . .
Oh
Oh
Oh
Oh
What?

She is in a state of death. Her energy is huge. She is concealed as

Miriam *elsewhere is revealed . . .*

Three: A mother

An old woman's living-room. Late morning. **Miriam**, *a woman in her late sixties, is standing. She is wearing a pinafore and has a cloth in her hand.*

Miriam Well, I don't know what to think.
I don't know what to do for t'best.
I've left back door oppen but I know it's not safe.
Anybody could just charge in.
Her up the road was in the same boat after she'd been painting her passage and someone walked in and walked off with her carriage clock.
But I know if I close it she's daft enough to think I'm at the shops or sommat and racket off again.
I'm worn out with it.

A **Fylgia** *brings on a chair for* **Miriam**. *Pause.* **Miriam** *looks at the chair arm. Picks at something with her finger nail. Polishes it in one spot.*

Miriam She's too long in t'tooth to be valliganting off.
She's always been too free and easy with people and whatnot.
'Isn't she friendly?'
Well, this is where Friendly gets you.
I thought she'd stopped this
Going Out Mullarkey.
But No.
She Was Born Under A Wandering Star.
I thought she might be with her three fences over but she says not.
'She normally comes in for a kiss and cuddle but she's been giving me the cold shoulder latterly.'
Well, she doesn't know who anybody is any more.
Except me.

She still knows her Mum.
Still loves her Mum.

Pause. Looks out of the window.

Raining now!
When she gets back it'll be Mud tracked all through.

She notices a mark on the window. Works on it with her cloth.

I'll have to put newspaper down.

Fylgia *gets newspaper.*

Miriam   No Rest for The Wicked.
I'm not having dirt.
Return of the Prodigal Daughter or no Return of the
Prodigal Daughter!
When Jack was alive he was in slippers minute he came
through that door!
Always went down to the shed to smoke.
Dirty clothes in Laundry Basket and no one leaving the
lavatory seat Up!
This one gets away with Blue Murder.
There'll be no sitting on settee till she's dried off!
There'll be a New Regime going when you decide to
pitch up again, lass!

She sits down on the chair to polish the legs. The **Fylgia** *moves
to* **John** . . .

Four: Suspicions

John, *a middle-aged man is sitting with a photograph album.*

John   I knew something was up
as soon as Spearmint Mouthwash started appearing in
the supermarket trolley.
And toothpaste for sensitive teeth.
She's never had sensitive teeth.
Sensitive nothing.

Up to press I've had to keep tabs on our dental
hygiene.
I saw Aquaminty and I thought 'There's someone else,
John lad.'
Then it's finding fault.
She's off canoodling and whatnot but it's me that
doesn't pass muster.
Decides I've got smelly feet.
I'm on Odour-Eaters all day and talcum powder before
I'm allowed in bed of a night!
Then I'm not allowed Peanut Brittle of an evening
because my crunching disturbs *Coronation Street*.
Big Economy Pack of Marshmallows appears.
I said 'It's like chewing mattresses.'
She says 'I wish Mavis would leave Derek.'
Then it's suddenly Lean Cuisines and Menu Masters.
I said 'What's this in aid of then?'
She said 'I'm slimming.'
I said 'I'm not.'
She said 'Pity.'
She goes to Marks and Spencer's,
says 'Do you want owt?'
I say 'I'm running low on underwear.'
She comes back with Boxer Shorts Extra Large.
I said 'Who Is He?'
She said 'No one you know. He drives an Astra GT.'
I said 'I'm moving into the spare bedroom then.'
She said 'You're not.
That's for guests.
You can use our Marie's sleeping bag.'
(*He looks at a photograph.*) She's not even smiling on this
wedding shot.

Five: The unbearable pain of parting

Two women . . . **Lily** *and* **Helen**. **Helen**, *in her coat, has
just arrived on a mercy dash.*

Lily   Oh.

Helen   Yes.

Lily   Oh Helen.

Helen   Yes.

Lily   Helen. Oh dear.

Helen   I know. I know.

Lily   Fuck her.

Helen   Yes.

Lily   She can just fuck right off!

Helen   Yes.
Is that what she's done?

Lily   Yes.
(*Quotes:*) 'I don't think it's working.'
'We both need space.'
'I need time alone.'
I hate her.

Helen   Me too.
I hate her.
Doing this to my friend.
I could kill her.
(*She hugs* **Lily** *efficiently.*) She's awful.

Lily   What's going on?
'I need to get away for a bit.'
That's a holiday, that's all that is! *WE* go on holidays!
We're good on holidays!
She can't afford it!
I looked at her bank statement.
What's going on?

Helen   Just a sticky patch.
Probably.

Lily   I miss her.

Fuck her.

Helen   Yes. Yes.
She'll ring.
You watch.

Lily   When she does . . . I'm not speaking to her!

Helen   Course you're not.
Shall we have a drink?

Lily   No.

Helen   Something to eat.
I'll make us something to eat.

Lily   No. I can't.
Everything tastes like cat shit.

Helen   Shall I heat up some cat shit?

Lily   Oh.
Do something.

Helen *maunders about. Arrives at music facility.*

Helen   Ah.
If music be the food of . . . (*Remembers the end of the
quotation.*)
Music?

Lily   Oh . . .

Helen *presses the button. Sinead O'Connor sings . . . 'Nothing
Compares To U'.*

Helen (*at intro . . . pleased*)   . . . Oh . . .

The lyrics are unfortunate. **Helen** *is embarassed.* **Lily** *listens as
tears roll down her cheeks.* **Helen** *switches off the music.*

Helen   Sorry.

Lily   I hate her fucking choice of music.
I don't want to be here.

Helen   Oh Lily.

Lily Everything's . . . hell. (*The word 'hell' has the requisite weight. She is in hell.*)
What shall I do?

Helen What do you want to do?

Lily Talk to her.

Helen Mmm. Ring her.

Lily She said she didn't want me to ring her.

They both think.

Both Fuck what she wants!

Lily *gets up.*

Lily I'll do it in the . . .

Helen Yeah.

Lily *exits.*

Helen *waits. The telephone by her pings. She waits.*

Lily (*off*) Fuck You Pick Up The Phone!
Pick It Up!
Fuck You And Your Ansaphone!
Where Are You?
Who Are You With?
Pick It Up!
Pick It . . . Fuck You!!!!

Helen *waits.*

Lily Help me, Helen.

Helen What do you want me to do?

Lily Make it better.

Helen (*to herself*) Get rid of her!

Six: Ten things to do in a hotel room

A hotel room somewhere. **Rachel** *appears in pyjama top.*

Rachel   Ten things to do in a hotel room.
One. Find the chocolate. (*She turns back the bed cover,
revealing the courtesy chocolate.*)
Two. Read it.
(*Reads:*) 'This bed has been prepared for your comfort by
Michelle.'
Thank you Michelle.
Three. Unwrap the chocolate. (*She does.*)
Four. (*She eats the chocolate.*)
Five. Feel remorse at eating the chocolate.
Hah.
Six. Try bed. (*She does.*)
Very nice, Michelle.
Seven. Anticipate. (*She stretches back.*)
Eight. (*She looks at watch, frowning.*)
Nine . . . make time speed by by reading erotic lesbian
literature . . . (*She reaches for her book . . . finds an appropriate
passage . . . reads.*)
. . . 'She pushed her back against her own door . . .'
Steady on.
'Taking her face in her hands she touched her lips in a
kiss which deepened widened softened hardened . . .'
Remarkably mobile features . . .
'Both lips parted and the tips of their tongues . . .
touched . . . (*She settles down more.*) . . . Then Jessica's hand
touched Carmel's breast lightly . . . (*She idly touches her own
breast.*) . . . featherlight touch . . . the nipple . . . grew
hard . . . (*She checks her nipple for hardness.*) . . . the two
bodies pressed into one another . . . (*Her hand moves down
below the bedclothes.*) They were kissing . . . holding each
other as if they would never ever ever let go of one
another . . . then Carmel's hand . . .' (*Her legs are drawn
up, her knees sticking up under the bedclothes. They part as . . .*)
Ten.

Seven: A dreadful morning

A woman's room. Late morning. **Joy** *comes in in dressing gown. She has an enormous hangover. A* **Fylgia** *with her has an enormous hangover too.*

Joy   Ooogh!

She walks out. Comes back with a bottle of aspirins.

Oh God!

She pours two or three or four onto her palm. While she is looking away, **Fylgia** *takes two, leaving just two.*

Joy   Christ!
(*She puts them in her mouth. With her mouth full:*) . . . Shit!

She walks out. **Fylgia** *eats its aspirins dry.*

Joy (*off*)   . . . Jesus, Mary and Joseph!

Comes back in with carton of milk, from which she is drinking. In the other hand she has a bottle of Lucozade. After drinking from the milk, she takes a slug of Lucozade.

God!
Well, what's made *you* so poorly?
Can't have been the gin and tonic at work, you only had one! (*Has a drink of milk.*)
Or the Chardonnay in the wine bar. 'I'm told the 1986 whites of the upper Loire valley are awflly good for their price!' Awflly.
What was his name? (*She drinks some Lucozade.*)
Robin.
Oh God!!!

She goes off, chucking her milk carton and Lucozade into the detritus drift.

(*Off.*) . . . Somebody put me out of my Misery!!!!

The **Fylgia***'s head lifts.* **Joy** *returns. This time she has a glass of water and a packet of 'Resolve'. She shakes the packet.*

Joy   Of course I should have stuck to white in the
restaurant but . . . (*Thinks for a moment.*) . . . Robin!!!!
insisted on red.
'White? With lamb????'
(*She reads the packet of Resolve.*) 'Beecham's Resolve is
effective when taken before retiring . . .'
Now You Tell Me!
(*She opens the packet. Pours it in the water. It fizzes. She reads
the packet.*) . . . 'Do not take other medicines containing
paracetamol while using Beecham's Resolve.'
Fuck off.
(*She stirs it with her finger.*) Tequila slammers at the party
might not have been a wise Career Move.
Followed by Sols beer.
Followed by a Trip to the Hostess's Lovely Bedroom for
a couple of lines off her highly polished dressing table.
Who had that? (*Thinks.*)
Simon Something.
Got me very lively anyway.
Enough to share my views on . . . ecology . . .
Fuck . . . with the guy who had the pony-tail and the
dope.
Who was that? (*Thinks.*)
Sky.
No.
No!
That was what was above me as I headed for the taxi.
That's when I started to feel dreadful.
That's what hit me.
The fresh fucking air.

Eight: The steamy rain forest

A sound of exotic bird song, insects. A **Fylgia** *comes on, treading
carefully. It keeps hearing a sound, looking back. Another* **Fylgia**
*comes on from the other side, treading carefully. It keeps hearing a
sound, looking back. They meet in the middle of a steamy rain*

forest. They sweat. One **Fylgia** *unwinds the long long long scarf from its neck. They get pestered by insects. Bitten. One pursues a flying insect and as it lands on the other* **Fylgia**, *it slaps at it. A squabble breaks out. Something lowers itself. It is a vine. One* **Fylgia** *swings on it. Something else lowers itself. The other* **Fylgia** *pulls on it. It comes down. It is a large snake. It has an apple in its mouth. This* **Fylgia** *wrestles it. The other* **Fylgia** *takes out a flask of tea. Pours tea into a cup. Sound of heart-rending sobbing.*

Nine: Late

Miriam's *room. Night time.* **Miriam** *standing by window.* **Fylgia** *brings her a cup of tea.*

Miriam   Still no news.
Wanderer hasn't returned.
I've had to lock up.
There's another Gay and Lesbian Disco on at the Pub.
Eee God.
Lasses screaming and lads peeing in doorways.
I've signed a petition but there's still goings-on down my back-passage.
(*She looks down at the cup.*) I don't remember mekking this.
She's never stayed out this late,
I don't know what to think.
I wish Jack was here.
I could have sent him out to look.
He used to say 'You care more about That One than you do about me.'
I'd say 'Don't be So Soft.'
He was a good man was Jack.
But he wasn't special.
This one is.
Somebody by Dustbins!
(*She peers.* **Fylgia** *peers.*)
That Bloody Tabby from the Garage!
Spraying Everywhere and dragging Kentucky Fried

Chicken out of Next Door's Bin.
Shoo, go on, get out!
Single Man.
Lot of Takeaways.
He should get himself married!
Keeps things Tidy!

Ten: Scissors

John *is cutting his wife's head out of all the photographs. The*
Fylgia *fretfully picks up the bits.*

John   Well, she's on her way tonight.
Going to live with 'Tony'.
Comes in last night with matching luggage from British
Home Stores.
I went out and got some Peanut Brittle and watched *The*
Vanishing World while she packed.
She said 'It sounds like somebody's walking on gravel.'
I said 'It's turtles dragging themselves up a beach in the
Galapagos Islands in *Vanishing World* so shut it!'
She said 'I'll take the photograph albums. Me Mam and
Dad paid for the wedding.'
Well, she's not wrong.
Little surprise when she shows these to Tony.
None of me in there.
That's what she wants.
She can have these of her.
White dress and veil.
Florist's spray.
And she'll have to be down at Marks and Spencer's first
thing tomorrow . . .
She's got no crotch left in any of her fancy knickers!

Eleven: The urge to couple is strong

Joy *arrives in her room. It is half an hour later. She is holding* *her dressing gown tightly round her.*

Joy   Oooohhhhh!

She walks out. Her **Fylgia** *runs about in a tizzy.*

(Off.) . . . OH God!!!!

She comes back on, her dressing gown held at the neck.

Oh Jesus!

She walks out again.

Oh Jesus Mary and Joseph!

She comes back in.

I'm covered in love bites!
All down my front!
From my neck to my knees!
I mean my knees!!!!
What about the back????

She rushes off again.

(Off.) . . . Oh God No . . . Yes!!!!

She comes back in and throws herself on the floor, curled in a heap. The **Fylgia** *rushes in, first with milk, then Lucozade, then aspirins, then Resolve.*

Joy   I don't even know who it was!
Fucked a fucking vampire and I can't remember!!!!
Fuck!
I'm hoping memory will return!
I'm hoping a clear memory of a condom's going to come flooding back!
I can't take any more of this!

Twelve: Nowhere

Mary, *nowhere, sensing all this. A* **Fylgia** *with her, waiting.*

Mary   Christ!
Jesus!
Oh My God!
Oh!
No!
No!
No!
No!
No . . . no . . . no.
Please.
Somebody.
(*Sees* **Fylgia**.) Oh!
(*Refuses to see* **Fylgia**.) Stay
stay stay stay
car my car stay in the car!
Fireworks!
Smell grease grease grease mechanic
welding cutting oh oh oh stay
police . . . police search
glove compartment
don't go!
Stay.
Come down
down down down stay down there.

Fylgia *reaches out hand.* **Mary** *snatches it away.*

Mary   Yes!
Yes!
Yes!
Come . . . down come
put together
keep it . . . together . . . oh
wrong . . . wrong wrong
What?
What?
early
diary fax paper paper fax
Mary Mary . . . oh

name name someone someone new
who
hotel hotel why where in two in two I'm in two
Yes!
Now! (*Looks at* **Fylgia**.)
Remember
No!!!!!!
Ooooooooooooooooh!

The **Fylgia** *takes her in its arms.* **Mary** *fights it.*

Mary   Please.
Somebody.
Oh!
Fuck!
Fuck No!
Please.
Help.
No.
Oh Dear Me.
This can't . . .
It isn't . . .
The Timing! Oh!
Oh no!
Inconvenient!
Inconceivable!
Shit!
Shit oh Shit!
The Mess.
Awful!
Awful!
The fucking awful mess!
Please!
Oh Please!

Fighting and fighting . . . She suddenly gives up.

Thirteen: Life defiantly continues

Lily*'s living room.* **Todd***, wearing a coat and gloves, is waiting for* **Lily** *to dress.*

Todd (*telling this to* **Lily***, who is off*)   . . . so he suggests retiring to His Place . . . I mean, Cliché . . . omitting to mention that His Place is in *Lower Sydenham*!!! Do you ever sense that your life is taking a Downward Spiral?

Lily (*off*)   Tell me about it!

Todd   Anyway, we drive interminable miles in THE FUEGO . . . which I bet you didn't know can go from 0 to 60 m.p.h. in fourteen point 38 seconds *flat* and handles very well on *bends* . . . until we pull up and go into this flat like Ian and Cindy's

Lily (*off*)   Who's Ian and Cindy?

Todd   in *EastEnders* . . . but there the Soap Opera nightmare doesn't end because sitting on one end of the SOFA BED . . . Ikea . . . is a Spooky Dead Ringer for GRANT MITCHELL who my pal introduces as 'My Boyfriend' who doesn't mind us doing it as long as HE CAN WATCH!!!!

Doorbell goes.

I'll get it!

Simultaneously **Todd** *gets to one side of the door,* **Helen** *to the other, as* **Lily** *appears at her bedroom door, hopeful, in clinging dress.*

Helen   Lily?

Todd   Mary?

Lily   Mary???

Helen   Helen.

Todd   Helen. Sorry.

Lily   HELEN.
(*Returns to her bedroom.*) Hi Helen.

Helen Hi!
How Are you?

Lily (*off*) Brilliant!

Helen (*sotto voce*) Any news of . . .

Todd Zilch.

Helen (*sotto voce*) How Is She?

Todd (*quoting, sotto voce*) . . . 'Fine.
Couldn't Be Better.
Feels Full Of Energy.
That Bitch Fucking Off Has Done Her A Favour.
She Feels Free. She Feels Strong.
She Just Wants To Get On With Her Life Now' . . .

Lily *appears, in high-heeled shoes, looking for her make-up bag.*

Helen Okay?

Lily Fine.
Couldn't be better.
I feel full of energy.
That bitch fucking off has done me a favour.
I feel free. I feel strong.
I just want to get on with the rest of my life now . . .

Exits.

Helen You look gorgeous.

Lily (*off*) What?

Helen (*embarrassed shout*) You Look Gorgeous!

Lily I've lost half a stone.

Helen What?

Todd She's lost half a stone.
It's An Ill Wind.
(*Sotto voce.*) I suspect a third party.

Helen (*sotto voce*) I suspect a third party.

Todd I like you.

Helen Oh. (*Stupid voice.*) Thank you very much. Thank you.

Todd (*sotto voce*) I never liked her.

Helen (*sotto voce*) Mary?

Todd (*sotto voce*) Mary!

Helen (*sotto voce*) I never liked her!

Todd (*sotto voce*) Get in there!

Helen (*sotto voce*) We're just friends!

Todd Oh.

Lily (*lipsticked, enters*) What are you two whispering about? (*She doesn't care.*)

Helen Nothing.

Sound of doorbell.

Todd Mini-cab!
(*To* **Lily**.) Get your cloak on, Cinders . . . Who knows but tonight, At The Ball . . .
(*To* **Helen**.) . . . I like you.
(*He kisses and hugs her.*) I want to meet you again. I'll get your number off Madam . . .
Lily . . . Glass Skates On!!!

He exits. **Lily** *puts on her coat.*

Lily It's a Party.
At Long Tall Sally's.
What I Really Feel Like! (*She doesn't.*)
Play The Field!
Meet Someone New!
Break Some Other Poor Fucker's Heart!
D'you want to come with . . .

Helen No.
No.

Just came to see how you were really!
If you're ... you know ... I'll ...

Lily   Sure?

Helen   Yeah.

Lily   Fuck.

Helen   Fuck.

Lily *hugs* **Helen**.

Helen   You smell nice.

Lily   You feel nice.
Warm. (*She disengages.*)
I'm so fucking *cold* all the time!

Todd *reappears.*

Lily   Mini-cab!
Yes, I'm coming!

Todd   No, it's not the mini-cab.
Sit down.

Fourteen: Ten things to do when you've been stood up

Rachel *arriving back at her home. She has her bag and her erotic lesbian novel.*

Rachel   Ten things to do when you've been stood up!
One. Expect a message! (*Switches on her ansaphone.*)

Ansaphone   'Rachel. S'Jimmy from Irene's Interiors.
I've got your six rolls of wallpaper that should do it.'
The Time announcement is off.

Rachel   I know it is.

Ansaphone   'Only Mother calling. Kitty's missing. Can you ... Oh I Hate This Thing!'

The Time announcement is off.

Rachel I know it is . . . I don't know how to work it . . .

Ansaphone 'Have you got a hairy cunt? I just want to fuck you!' (*Obscene caller comes.*)
The Time announcement is off.

Rachel Nice one, vicar.

Ansaphone 'Hello doll. S'Nicky here. How's it going? Is She Good? Is it Lerv? Awaiting details. Sordider the better nyeh nyeh nyeh! With diagrams! Nyeh nyeh nyeh! Bye now!'
The Time announcement is off. That was your last message.

Rachel Two!

Rachel *hurls her novel to the floor in rage.* **Rachel** *hurls her bag to the floor in rage.*

Three!
Four!

She dials a number.

Hello. (*Very angry.*)
This is your secret weekend date.
Again.
Wondering what's happened to you.
Cold feet?
Unavoidably detained?
Second thoughts?
I await your explanation with Bated Breath.
(*Thinks.*)
You owe me one half of a very expensive hotel bill you bastard.
Oh.
This is Rachel Stoker.
We went to bed together.
The earth moved.

(*Puts phone down. Redials.*) Fuck you.
(*Puts phone down. Redials.*) Of course, if something dreadful
has happened to you, she found out ha ha, ring me.
It's Rachel. (*Phone down.*)
Five. Nice cup of tea.
Six. (*Brings out Mars Bar.*)
Seven.
Aaaaaaaaaaaaaaaaagh!
Eight. Remember to breathe.
Shit!
(*Redials.*) Mary, wipe these messages as soon as you get
in.
Fuck.
Sorry.
Oh dear. (*Puts phone down.*)
Oh dear, oh dear, oh dear.

Fifteen: The briny ocean

A **Fylgia** *comes rowing on in a tiny makeshift boat. The ocean
roars and sprays. The boat rides the tossing waves. The* **Fylgia**
*goes from smiling to very very seasick. It takes some 'Resolve'. The
sea gets calmer. It decides to fish. Reels in a second* **Fylgia**, *who
has been snorkelling. They put makeshift snorkel, flippers, air-bottle
on the* **Fylgia** *in the boat. They both dive. They encounter shoals
of fish, sea-horse, an octopus. They capture a large shark. They
put a hand in the shark and start bringing out what is in its
stomach . . . a car bumper, a tin of salmon, one of* **Lily**'s *high-
heeled shoes, a chocolate each, a black and white cat . . .*

Sixteen: Advertising

Miriam's *room. Daytime.*

Miriam   I've put a postcard up in the Paper Shop.
Mr Battergee read it as he put it in the window,
said he'd keep an eye out for her.

He's got an Alsatian.
Reckons to be a Guard Dog but it eats Hoola-Hoops.
And I've stuck notices on the trees down Fulford
Avenue.
I've caught her coming back from there, smelling of fish.
She'll come waltzing in saying 'I'd like some chicken,
Mum
or a bit of lightly done liver.'
I think she's got lost somewhere and someone's taken
her in.
She can sit on the settee if she wants.
When she comes back.
I don't mind.
(*Pause. Suddenly.*) It was my fault she went.
I went into the bathroom
and there in the middle of the bath
great big dollop of S-H-one-T.
I saw red.
She knows how I like things nice.
It takes me nearly two days these days to get round.
Get all done.
But if they catch you getting dirty they think you can't
manage and they put you in Grange House and you
have to sit in shiny yellow chairs in rows wi' a lot of old
lasses that want to watch rubbish and you get folk like
Marie Tunnicliffe from Church singing 'We'll Gather
Lilacs' at you.
I said 'Where are you?'
She was sitting on the settee
and I gave her a great wallop,
I don't know what came over me.
I blame television.
She shot out.
I've never hit an animal before.

Seventeen: Speaking clock

John's *house. He is winding up an alarm clock.*

John   I've moved over her side of the bed.
I'm enjoying the benefit of the bedside table.
When she comes crawling back she can try balancing
her cocoa mug on the laundry basket!
She's off with Tony on a Winter Break in Lanzarote.
'He takes me places.
He spends money.'
We'll see how much he likes spending money . . . I
nipped over to take her letters . . .
Caretaker let me in.
Told him I was her brother.
When they get back after two weeks they're going to be
greeted by a voice from his green telephone . . .
'The time in Sydney is three fifteen and forty
seconds . . .
the time in Sydney is three fifteen and fifty seconds . . .
the time in Sydney is three sixteen precisely.'

Eighteen: Memory

Joy *storms in, dressed in coat.*

Joy   Oooooooogh!

Hurls down her car keys, walks out.

(*Off.*) . . . Oh God!

She storms back in.

Jesus!
I've lost my bloody car.

Storms out again.

(*Off.*) . . . Jesus, Mary and Joseph!

*Comes back with an empty packet of cigarettes. Hurls it to the
floor.*

God in Heaven!

Walks out again. Returns again with a waste-paper basket stuffed with rubbish. Upends it on the floor. **Fylgia** *watches. One, specifically.* **Joy***, on hands and knees, sorts through the detritus.*

Joy   Aha!

Holds up a cigarette butt. Which is one third smoked. Puts it in her mouth. Searches her coat pockets for matches.

Went to the road I *thought* I'd left it.
Nothing! Zip! Zero!
Dammit to buggery if it's been stolen!
To Buggery!

Fylgia *starts picking up the rubbish, listening with polite concern.*

Joy   It's *supposed* to go Beep beep ner-ner ner-ner if it's attacked.
But it only does that to *me* when I'm late for sodding work!!!
(*She lights the butt. Takes a drag.*) OOOOooooh . . . God!

Gags and throws the lighted cigarette into the waste-paper basket which the **Fylgia** *has just collected.* **Fylgia** *frantically scrabbles to stop the fire.*

Joy   I did take the car to the party.
Didn't I?
Did I? (*She tries to remember.*)
Did I drive?

The possibilities that she totalled the car, knocked someone over, etc., etc., occur to her. She looks at the book of matches, turns it over, reads.

'Rumours Cocktail Lounge.
Wellington Street.'
When the fuck did I go there?
(*Reads other side.*) 'Happy Hour 5 til' 7.'
(*She thinks.*) After the wine bar.
Harvey Wallbangers.

With . . . (*She thinks.*)
Harvey?

She buries her head in rubbish.

Nineteen: A good night's sleep

Lily *is in bed asleep. Sinead O'Connor sings 'I Am Stretched on Your Grave'. The telephone rings.* **Lily** *wakes up abruptly. Picks it up.*

Lily   Mary?
Dad!
Sorry . . . I was dreaming.
I was dreaming.
I . . . (*She bursts into tears.*)
Just a minute, Dad. (*She cries. Pulls a lot of tissues out of a box.*)
Shit.
Shit.
Shit shit shit. (*Blows her nose.*)
Stop. Okay. Stop.
Okay. (*Picks up phone again.*)
Dad.
Sorry.
I was dreaming somebody was alive and I woke up and they were . . . (*She starts crying again.*)
What?
Yes, I'm upset.
Yes.
Yes.
Yes.
Mary.
With the short brow . . .
Yes.
You have.
You did.

At the pub I took . . .
Yes.
That one.
A car crash.
Yes.
What.
Nissan Micra.
Yes . . . it . . .
The M4.
Yes . . . it is a bad . . .
I don't know which junction.
Yes.
Thank you.
No, I'm . . .
Saturday.
Cremated. (*Her face crumples.*)
Hang on.

Puts phone down. Takes deep breath. Picks up phone.

She was my lover, Dad.
My lover.
I'm feeling so . . . bad.
I can't tell you but it's probably just a phase I'm going
through.
Yes, it is probably nearly as bad as losing a husband or
a wife, yes.
I'm in pieces. (*She smiles.*)
So is she.
The M4.
I don't know which turn-off.
Car's a write-off but what can you expect if you don't
buy British!!!

Pause.

Dad, I'm sorry.
I've just woken up.
I don't know what I'm saying.
How's Mum?

Twenty: Ten pieces of crockery

*Outside **Rachel***'s *house. Very early dawn.* **Rachel** *comes out, carrying a variety of mugs and plates. She puts them down on the grass. There is a high wall in front of her, away from the audience. She starts throwing the crockery, piece by piece, at the wall.*

Rachel   One!
Two!
Three!
Four!

A dog barks frantically.

Fuck off!
Five!
Six!

Sound of a window opening.

Seven.

Voice (*off*)   What the fuck are you doing?

Rachel   Fuck off.
Eight.
Nine.
Just fuck right off!
Just fuck right off will you?
Just fucking fuck right off will you!
Ten!
Ten!
Ten!
Ten!
Quiet now.
Sorry.
You can all go back to sleep.

Twenty-one: All my worldly gifts

John *is dismantling the alarm clock.*

John   I don't know how Switzerland gets on now it's
all digital watches.
I suppose they concentrate on the Winter Sports side of
the Economy.
That's where they're going for their honeymoon.
I said 'I thought you'd been having that for the past
year.'
She said 'Not everybody thinks a honeymoon means
watching Cricket Week in Scarborough.'
She's wearing Sweat Bands.
I said 'Is that Après Ski then?'
She said 'I've been Working Out.'
I said 'Is that what they're calling it now?'
She said 'It's Leisure . . .
There's more to Leisure than Peanut Brittle and I want
a divorce and I want half of everything.'
'Fair enough' I said.
I've dismantled the bed.
That's in two pieces.
I've painted a white line from storage loft to cellar.
Seven forty-five I take delivery of a chain saw from
Industrial Machines Hire on Carpenters Road.
She wants half the Metro she can have the passenger
side.
My Mam gave us this clock but I'm not stingy.

The clock comes into two distinct halves.

She can have one while six or six while twelve, I don't
care!

Twenty-two: News

Miriam's *room. She is sitting in her chair.*

Miriam   I was watching *Home and Away.*
Phone goes.

I wasn't expecting anyone.
It wasn't Sunday.
Woman's voice.
'Hello, you don't know me but are you the owner of the
big black and white cat only I got your number off of
the trees.'
I said yes.
I sat down.
She said 'Only I'm sorry to tell you but I think I've
seen her lying in the gutter outside the Housing Offices
in Rottingdean Road.
I'm ever so sorry.'
I said When was this.
She said Yesterday.
She said she thought she recognised her because she
used to remind her of a cat of hers.
I went down.
State of road cleaning these days you'd have thought
she'd still have been there,
but no
I walked up and down looking.
Nothing.
Rastafarian lad came by, can of beer.
Said 'Looking for dog ends missus??'
I said, 'My cat's been run over. She's supposed to be
here, but I think she's been taken away.'
He offers me his can.
I have a swig.
Broad daylight!
He said 'I'm very sorry.
What was her name?'
I said 'Kitty.'

She starts to cry quietly.

Twenty-three: Popular

Joy's *flat. A* **Fylgia** *is holding the base of the telephone.* **Joy** *has the receiver. She puts it down.*

Joy Oooooooogh!

She walks off.

(Off.) Oh God!

Walks back with large bag of crisps. Opens them angrily.

Jesus, Mary and Joseph!

Eats one or two. Walks off.

(Off.) . . . Jesus!

Comes back with jar of mayonnaise. Dips crisps in and eats them.

Well, it seems I won't be invited back to her house for a while.
Someone was sick in her Weeping Fig and I'm Prime Suspect One.
I denied it.
I said I was sick in your bidet.
I was sick on your shoes.
I was sick in my own Weeping Fig but I swear on my mother's grave that the contents of my stomach stayed in situ in your sodding Victorian-style conservatory!
She's not having any of it.
She made mention of cigarette butts in the avocado dip. *(Thinks.)* That was me.
She claims I didn't arrive in my car.
I was with someone who didn't speak any language anybody could put a finger on but bowed and stroked me a lot with his many-ringed hands!
Who the sweet Jesus was that? *(Tears start in her eyes.)*
I'm a bit of a mess, me.

Twenty-four: Smoke gets in your eyes

Helen *and* **Todd** *in black coats somewhere in the vicinity of a crematorium. Both take out packets of ten cigarettes . . . take one out. Light up. They inhale.*

Todd   I don't smoke any more.

Helen   Neither do I.

They smoke.

Todd   I loathe this crematorium.
I'm here more often than Safeways.

Helen *pats his hand.*

Todd   People I've seen off here . . . past few years . . . Jeff . . . Camp Colin . . . both Peters . . . Phelim . . . that little Cornish queen with the very blue eyes . . . name's gone . . . William! . . . William . . . Roger Pritt . . . John Call-Me-Mary-Dixon . . . I have to say it makes a nice change it being a woman this time.

Helen   Nice change.

Todd   Oh shut up.
I don't have to be nice.
I'm living on borrowed time.

Helen   The nicer you are now, the better crowd you'll get at the end of the day.

Todd   Short day.

Helen   Good-looking corpse.

They hold hands.

Todd   Where's Lily?

Helen   With Mary's parents.

Todd   Christ. In-laws at last.

Helen   They're quite nice.
They're busy bonding with the various members of the

community their daughter omitted to mention she belonged to.

Todd   'The nicer you are now . . . the better crowd you'll get at the end of the . . .'

Helen   Oh shut up.

They smoke and stare.

Helen   What d'you think happens?

Todd   After? Ham and tongue sandwiches!

Helen   No! EDGAR LUSTGARDEN . . . 'Afffff . . . Terrrr.'

Todd   Fuck Knows.
I'm hoping for a Gay Disco.
Like 'Heaven'.
You?

Helen   Nice library.
Get well-read.

Todd   No sex?

Helen   God no.

They smoke and stare.

Todd   Lovely day for it.

Helen   Warm for the time of year.
Blue sky.
Sun.

They stare.

Helen (*looking*)   Fuck.
Look.

Todd   What.

Helen   From the chimney.
Smoke.
Is that . . . ?

Todd   Mary.
Oh yes.

Helen   Well, everybody's smoking.

They both start laughing, horrified at themselves. **Rachel** *enters.*

Helen   Shhhhh!
No . . .
look . . .
stop . . .
it isn't . . .

Todd *is turned away. She hits him on the back.*

Helen   He's hysterical with grief.

Rachel   I'm sorry . . .
Are you a friend of Mary's?

Helen   Sort of . . . I'm more a . . .

Rachel   I really need to talk to someone who . . .

Helen   . . . friend of Lily's.

Rachel   . . . knew her . . .

Helen   Well, perhaps you should . . .

Rachel   Mary . . .

Helen   . . . talk to Lily . . . if she's . . .

Rachel   No. Not Lily.

Helen   No.

Rachel   I mustn't talk to Lily.
No.

Helen   Oh.

Todd   Talk to us.
You can talk to us.

Twenty-five: Mary's room

The lights rise to reveal **Mary** *standing in her room. Eyes closed.*

Mary   Here!
Here! home!
now
home
please
home
home
yes yes yes yes
Yes!

She opens her eyes but can see nothing. Fumbles to a chair. Sits down but can feel nothing. Shakes her head wildly. A key turns in a lock . . . she does not hear it. **Lily** *enters. She stands in the doorway.* **Mary** *does not look round. Her head, however, lifts.*

Mary   Lily.

Lily *looks round.*

Lily   Oh.

Mary   Lily.

Lily *moves to behind the comfortable chair.*

Mary   Oh Lily.

Mary *gets up as* **Lily** *sits in the chair.*

Lily   Oh dear.

Mary *watches* **Lily**. **Lily** *sits in the chair, puts her hands on its arms, rubs her hands up and down the arms.*

Mary   Lily.

Lily   Oh dear me oh dear me oh dear.

Mary   Lily.

Lily *looks down. Head in hands. In the chair she sees something. Takes it out. It is the other glove to the one* **Mary** *wears. Both look at their separate gloves.*

Lily   Mary.

Mary   Oh Lily. Oh dear.

Lily *puts on the glove. She wipes tears from her eyes. She puts the gloved hand between her legs, holding ever harder and tighter. Her legs twist and wrap round her arm.*

Mary   Lily . . .
Just . . .

Lily   Mary.
Oh Mary. Talk to me.

Act Two

Twenty-six: New Year

Joy's flat. She is sitting curled up. She is drinking a whisky and holding an unlit cigarette. A **Fylgia** listens.

Joy Right!
End of the year soon
New Start.
Get myself . . .
a new personality.
Resolutions.
(*She takes a sip of whisky.*) No more drinking.
(*Thinks.*) To Excess.
(*Contemplates cigarette.*) Absolutely no smoking.
Recreational drugs.
Just say no.
(*Drinks some whisky.*) Healthy diet.
Frugal.
Lightly steamed vegetables.
Brown rice.
Aqua Libra. (*She grimaces, drinks more whisky.*)
Save The Planet.
Work for others.
Not myself.
Be nicer.
Better.
Popular.

She puts the cigarette in her mouth. Draws on it. Looks at it. Takes out her book of matches. She stands up and walks into the next scene with a cigarette in her mouth. As she goes she picks up a 'Pass the Pigs' box.

Twenty-seven: A game of chance

Helen, **Todd** *and* **Joy** *are at* **Lily**'s. *As* **Joy** *enters with cigarette* **Helen** *and* **Todd** *shout* '*NO*'. **Joy** *puts cigarette out. They are playing* '*Pass the Pigs*'. *They each have a beer bottle or can, some empties about. There is a big bowl of Quavers into which they dip.*

Todd   Come on piggies, make my day!

Joy (*reading box*)   . . . 'The original game of chance using pigs as dice.'

Todd   One of them's on its feet. What's that?

Helen/Joy   Single trotter. Five points.

Todd *throws.*

Helen/Joy   Pig Out! Pass the Pigs!

Todd   Why don't we play that 'ten' thing?

Joy   What ten thing?

Todd   Name ten types of pasta . . . name ten makes of car . . .

Helen   Oh right. Mary's game.

Todd   Ah. Pigs.

Joy (*reading*)   . . . 'After all, pigs are lucky and pigs have class' . . . Hmmm.

She takes a handful of Quavers. Swills some beer.

Helen   Double Leaning Jowler!
Double Leaning Jowler! Yyyyyyyessssssssss!
How many's a Double Leaning Jowler, Joy?

Joy (*reading*)   'Double Leaning Jowler . . . sixty points!'

Todd   What's a Double Leaning Jowler?

Joy *and* **Helen** *show him.*

Helen   It's just your little front trotters . . .

Joy   . . . and a little lean on your jowl . . .

Both   See?

There is a sound of a key in a lock.

Todd   Lily!

A flurry of activity . . . empties cleared, 'Pass the Pigs' picked up. The beer and Quavers cleared. **Joy** *manages to keep a bottle of something and a bowl of Quavers. They are suitably grave and sorrowful when* **Lily** *comes in.*

Todd   Hi Toots.

Helen   Where've you been, you look . . .

Joy   Sweetheart!
Nice drink? Something to eat?
Lovely hot deep bath?
Oils? Neroli? Rosemary!
Sandalwood!

Lily (*hands something to* **Todd**)   Put this on.

Joy   Music.
Yessss!

Helen   What is it?

Lily   Listen.

Tape   'Fuck You Pick Up The Phone!
Pick it Up!
Fuck You And Your Ansaphone!
Where Are You?
Who Are You With?
Pick It Up!
Pick It . . . Fuck You!!!!'
BEEP.

Joy (*listening intently*)   . . . That's you, isn't it?
It's Lil!

Lily   Yes.
That's me.
Listen.

Tape   'It's Mummy . . . just to say I couldn't get the wool in black, but they've got it in charcoal . . . it's quite dark . . . what d'you think? . . . Oh, it's Mummy by the way . . . did I say that . . . anyway Mummy . . .'
BEEP.

Todd (*to* **Joy**)   . . . That's Mummy.

Helen   Lil . . .

Lily   Shhh!

Tape   'Hello.
This is your secret weekend date.
Wondering what's happened to you.
Cold feet?
Unavoidably detained?
Second thoughts?
I await your reply with
Bated Breath.'
BEEP.

Joy   Who's that?

Lily   Listen!

Tape   'You owe me one half of a very expensive hotel bill you bastard.
Oh.
This is Rachel Stoker.
We went to bed together.
The earth moved.'
BEEP.

Joy   Who's Rachel Stoker?

Todd/Helen   Shhh!

Tape   'Fuck you'.
BEEP.

Helen   Todd ... (*Puts the tape off.*)

Lily   Leave it!

Tape   'Of course, if something dreadful's happened to you, she found out ha ha, ring me.
It's Rachel.'
BEEP.

Helen   Oh dear.

Tape   'Mary, wipe these messages as soon as you get in.
Fuck.
Sorry.
Oh dear.'
BEEP.

Joy   Who's Rachel Stoker?

Todd   It was probably a wrong number!

Lily   Who's Rachel Stoker?

Todd   I swear on my mother's grave I don't know anyone called ...

Lily (*to* **Helen**)   ... Who's Rachel Stoker?

Helen   Shit.
She works ... worked with Mary.
She was at the funeral.
We ... she spoke to us ...
They'd just started ...
Lil ... this isn't worth ...

Lily *starts collecting clothes and belongings and dumping them on the three of them.*

Lily   Out.
Get out.
Go.

Helen   It didn't seem ... there was no point telling you ...

Lily   This your coat?

Helen   You know it isn't!
Lily . . .

Todd   Come on, Helen . . . we need to go . . .

Joy   Let's have a drink! A drink's what we all need! All get wrecked, yeah?
Look . . . snacks . . .

Joy *has been shoved out with the Quavers.*

Hey, hey, The Bowl's *yours* Sweetheart!

Lily   Keep it.
Out.
Goodbye.

Helen   Oh Lily, for fuck's sake!

Lily (*losing it*)   . . . Liars!
Lying to Me!
You've Been Lying To Me!
Why does Everybody Lie To Me????

She has pushed them all outside. They are half in their coats. **Joy** *still has the bowl of Quavers.*

Twenty-eight: My apple tree, my brightness

Lily's *room. We hear outside . . .*

Helen   Lily . . . come on . . . Lily . . .

Todd   We can talk about this!
Can we talk about this?
Why don't we talk about this?

Joy   Lily . . . This Is Your Bowl!
Let's have a Drinkkkk . . .
Bloody Lesbians!
(*To others.*) Let's go have a drink and fuck her!

The lights fade as their voices fade. **Lily** *crosses to the music.*
Takes tape out and holds it like a poisoned thing. **Mary** *enters*
and puts on another tape. It is the last verse of 'I Am Stretched
On Your Grave' sung by Sinead O'Connor. Both listen. As it goes
into the reel, both start to speak. The speeches are delivered
together. Neither listens to the other. Each is too busy justifying to
listen . . .

Mary   I was going to tell you I was going to it wasn't
that I was lying it was just it was very early almost too
early and it was mine/it was just mine mine alone see
. . . everything, everything everything was ours . . .
everything was shared
shared shared shared

Lily   Liar
Liar
Liar
You lie about everything
it all comes out of your mouth
yarbly yarbly yarbly
but it's all lies all fucking lies

Mary   You never said 'I' you never said 'you'
it was always 'we'
what are we doing where are we going
of course we'll come I mean if I'd wanted to get
married . . .

Lily   I love you
don't give me that
don't say that oh don't even think it
when you're out at work . . . an affair at work . . . oh
please . . . tacky talk about tacky/ . . . every word you
say is a big fat lie was a big fat lie and I hate you I
fucking hate you . . .

Mary   It was like being in somebody else's sledge!
whizzing along lovely trees lovely snow lovely ice lovely
frozen lake and I'm all wrapped up in fur and it's warm
and snug and/yet and yet I want to stop and get out . . .

Lily   I'm glad you're dead
I'm glad
You deserve to die
Liar
What happened to let's experience everything together
eh eh
garbage your usual garbage
like I've given up smoking I've given up drinking no I
haven't been flirting me no/ I told you I love you
garbage
garbage

Mary   This is partly your fault you know!
It is oh it is!
This wasn't all me.
Oh no.
This is you too you know./
Oh yes
Oh yes

Lily   The waste of my time!
The waste
The pathetic miserable waste
On you/
On you
Christ!
Christ!

Mary   I mean when was the last time we had good
sex I mean really really good sex?/You can't remember
I can't remember. Nobody can remember. Doing it
because we meant it. Not anything athletic. Just real.
Just really touching each other

Lily   I've even got to be humiliated over your death.
You fuck pig.
You can't even keep that clean can you, can you?
/Humiliate me with my friends!

Why couldn't you ever be clear?

Airy fairy woolly cotton wool flannel words!

Mary   And Talking.
Let's talk about talking.
You just say oh don't start arguing Mary nobody wants
to argue with you
Verbal diarrhoea well/I just wanted to get a reaction
that's all

And I'm not lazy.
Don't say I'm lazy.
Don't ever say I'm lazy

Lily   I hope you're in hell
I hope you fry
I hope you
I hope you
I hope you
Oh God!

Mary   I wanted to get cold I wanted to get hurt I
wanted to take my gloves off and watch my hands turn
blue/
I wanted to get frostbite
Frostbitten

Lily   I hate the music you play
I hate your friends
I hated that coat you got
but I didn't lie did I?
Do you like it you said?
No I said/
You'd have lied oh yes Lily
It's beautiful you're beautiful
I love you
Liar

Liar

Mary   And you're going to say what has she got that I
wasn't providing? And it was nothing nothing nothing

except . . . except it wasn't you do you understand that
. . . I don't think you'd understand that you'll say/

Lily   Liar

Mary   I don't understand what you're saying speak in
descriptions!
Be honest be honest weren't you feeling something was
wrong weren't you?
Thinking aaagh get a bomb under this/pile of stagnant
compost
let's blow the pile of crap away
see what's under there?

Lily   Everything was good was solid was right
was nothing wrong with it
stability
a good relationship
security/
and you just decided to snap your fingers and pooffff!

Mary   Lily Lily I loved you but it was all going . . .
I've resisted loads of times no I'm faithful and this time
this time I didn't even think/ . . . that must be indicative
mustn't it . . . my brain was like oh fudge so my heart
just took over . . .

Lily   Why couldn't you think?
Why?
What you were doing
Where it would leave us
Leave me/
Didn't you care?

Mary   I didn't know what was going to happen
very little had happened
hardly anything compared to you and me
hardly anything/

Lily   Liar

Killer

Wrecker

Where are you?

Your Mess here!

Liar!

Mary   So stupid
So fucking stupid
Everything's so stupid
I don't know what to say
I'm speechless
You take away my words
Black hole

*They are both exhausted. Neither has listened to the other. A
dreadful, large, black hole appears which they both regard with
horror.*

Lily   That's it, Mary.
That's it.

Mary *watches as* **Lily** *goes to the phone.*

Lily   Hello.
Helen.
It's okay.
Listen.
You must have this Rachel Stoker's number . . .

Twenty-nine: Death's dominion

Miriam*'s room. She has got on a coat, handbag, smart hat.*

Miriam   I've just come back from Bournemouth!
Well, just outside.
Her three fences over knocked, said 'I hope you don't
think I'm butting in . . . but I found this in my Bill's
drawer!'
Article about a Pet Cemetery.
'Pets At Peace.'

I wrote.
Very nice letter back.
Mister Phillips.
Director.
Paid his respects and said No, it didn't matter that I
didn't have the deceased's remains, I could still purchase
a plot and headstone.
I went down.
Lovely peaceful place.
Grass.
Gravel walks.
Kitty's grave is in D86.
Marble Headstone.
'Kitty.
Beloved Companion of Miriam.
1992–1999.'
Flower Holder.
I took roses.
Bit of laurel.
Grey gravelly bits in a stone border.
I said 'Well old lass, don't say I don't do you proud!'
Better phone our Rachel in a minute.
(*Reading the paper.*) . . . Guide Dog's got run over in New
York. America.
Received one thousand four hundred Get Well Cards.
His owner, a Blind Man, received five cards.
People are Kind.

Pause.

Oh, I do miss her.
(*Looks at the newspaper.*) Thirty-first of December.
New Year.
You can keep it!

Thirty: Mountain landscape

Two **Fylgias** *climbing a mountain. Wild sky with clouds behind.*

They are carrying a baby which they pass to each other. They reach the dreadful black hole. They are listening very hard. It is very windy. A sound as of gas escaping. A mist rolls in. They put on party hats, party streamers. The baby gets a hat. They listen to Sinead O'Connor singing 'It's been so lonely without u here' from 'Nothing Compares To U'.

Thirty-one: You cause as much sorrow

Lights fade as song continues . . .

Lights to reveal the end of a very sticky evening involving **Todd**, **Helen**, **Joy** *and* **Rachel** *at* **Lily**'s. *Everybody here is wearing party hats and streamers.*

Rachel   Well, I think I'd better . . .

As she gets up, **Todd** *and* **Helen** *leap to also, with unseemly haste.* **Joy**, *who is drunk, is happy to stay for ever.*

Todd/Helen   Yes, I think we'd all better . . .

They run like stags for the coats.

Lily   Good to meet you.
Under the circumstances.

Rachel   Yes. Yes.

Joy (*sincere drunk*)   . . . You'll understand when you have chilren . . . you see the thing is none of you have chilren so you doan unnerstan . . .

Todd   It's a collection of pervs and wooftas . . . course we don't understand.

Joy (*hitting him good-naturedly . . . raucous drunk*)   . . . I doan mean that! You're so funny! He's so funny! I love you I really do!

Todd   I'm a happy man. Now I can die happy.

Joy (*sincere drunk*)   . . . I mean iss the creation of it . . .

iss the creative act of . . . of bringing these little . . .
creations . . . into the world . . . thass wass so creative . . .
thass wass so very creative . . . (*Sincere drunk has turned over
the speech to sentimental drunk. She cries movingly.*)

Todd   Can you be creative with this coat, dear?

Lily   Joy . . . put your fucking coat on and fuck off out
of here!

Joy (*arms round* **Lily**)   . . . This iss my bess frien . . . I
love her. I do. Her lover died. Give me a kiss.

Lily   No.

Joy   Yes.

Lily   No.

Joy   Yes.

Todd   Give her a kiss.
I'll drag her out while she's swooning.

Lily *kisses* **Joy** *on the lips. A passionate drunk from* **Joy**.

Joy   I can see what you lot see in it. I can see it.

Lily   Goodnight, Joy.

Todd *pulls her out.*

Joy   I can see it.

Lily   Fuck off.

Joy   I can see it!

Todd *and* **Joy** *have exited.*

Lily   That's my best friend.
I love her for her quiet manners and noble dignity.

Rachel   You've known her a long time.

Lily   Yes.

Helen   Well . . . (*She goes to the bedroom.*) . . . mini-cab

... shall I ... ?

Rachel   Please.

Helen *exits.*

Rachel   Helen's nice.

Lily   Yes.

Rachel   Were you two ever ... ?

Lily   No!
She's a friend.

Rachel   You don't er ... with friends?

Lily   No.
Just with lovers.

Rachel   Look, I don't think this was a very good id ...

Lily   You're very pretty.
I'd like to kiss you.

Rachel   Oh.

Lily   I've wanted to all evening.

Rachel   Yes. Yes.

Lily *kisses* **Rachel**.

Rachel   This is strange ...

Lily   Yes.

She kisses **Rachel** *again.* **Helen** *comes out of the bedroom.*

Helen   Oh.
Rachel, your cab's waiting outs ...
Do you want to ...
Well, up to you!

Lily   Helen, you take it.

Helen   Oh. Well. Right.

Lily *kisses her.*

Helen   Lily . . .

Lily   Take care.
Bye.

Helen   Bye.
Bye.

She exits.

Rachel   Well.

Lily   Well.

Rachel   Better be . . .

Lily   Yes . . .

Rachel   Night then.

Lily   Night.

Rachel   I'm not drunk enough.

Lily   You don't have to be drunk.

She gets hold of **Rachel** *by the coat and pulls her to her and kisses her soundly. Both pull back.*

Rachel   What's this about?

Lily   Life!

They seize each other. They are kissing. **Lily** *is unbuttoning* **Rachel**'s *coat,* **Rachel** *is unbuttoning* **Lily**'s *shirt. They are touching each other more and more intimately and fiercely as Sinead O'Connor sings 'You Cause As Much Sorrow'. Lights fade with the music.*

Thirty-two: A street

Helen *with her keys, having left the mini-cab, about to go into her house.*

Helen (*off*)   Ten quid?

Ten quid?
It's seven fifty it's always seven fifty
You f . . .
Late-night girl don't start a fight!
(*Sound of car door slamming.*) And a happy bloody New
Year to you!

Enters, purse open, in a rage.

New!
New!
New?
What's new about it?
Everything's old fucking old!
Here's how it works!
It doesn't!
Here's what's fair about it . . .
Nothing!
Lily! (*She makes her keys into a knuckle-duster and jabs them in
a pair of make-believe eyes.*)
How could you get it so wrong????
People love you, you know!
They *love* you!

Goes in through her door.

AAAaaaaaaaaaaaaagh!!!!

Comes out. Unnatural calm.

Well, I've been burgled!
Thank you God!

Thirty-three: A toilet experience

Joy's *room.* **Todd** *looking idly about.*

Joy   Oh God!
(*Sound of immense vomiting.*) Vreeeaaaauuuurgh!
Oh Jesus!
Yeeeaaaauuuurgh!

Jesus, Mary and Joseph!
Urgh . . . ugh . . . eeegh.

Appears with a towel, with which she is wiping herself.

Okay, okay, okay.
World's stopped spinning.
I feel like Death!
How about you?

Todd   I feel like going home.

Joy   Don't go home!
Why do you want to go home?

Todd   Because I feel like Death.

Joy   You should look after yourself, you.

Todd   You should look after yourself, you.

Joy   Why?
What's the point?

Todd   Life's precious.

Joy   I know.
But it's fucking awful too. (*She starts crying.*)
I wish I didn't dream!

Todd   Tell me about having children.

Thirty-four: Senile

Miriam's *room. She is asleep in her chair. A* **Fylgia** *comes and crawls into her lap.*

Miriam (*eyes closed*)   Kitty! Puss . . . puss . . .
Rachel?
(*Opens her eyes.*) Oh!
(*She sees the* **Fylgia**. *She smiles at it.*) Aw!
(*She sees it is really there.*) Crikey!
(*She sits up straight. She blinks.*) Go away!

Go on . . . Scram!
I'm not having this, no!
Is it you, Jack?
(*She looks.*) Jack?
Renee Whitburn from Cedar Road thought four men
were living with her when she went senile, sleeping with
her in her bed. She were laughing and wearing a lacy
nightie when they took her to General Infirmary.
I'm going daft, aren't I?

Fylgia *shakes its head.*

I can't manage by myself
I'll have to be enrolled at Grange House, won't I?

Fylgia *shakes its head.*

Are you God or sommat?

Fylgia *smiles and shakes its head.*

Who the bugger are you?

Thirty-five: Intruder

John'*s room. He is standing stock still, listening hard.*

John (*strangulated whisper*) I'm a bit sorry I never sorted
out the sneck on the lavatory window!
Somebody's In The House!
This is what you get for stinting on Domestic Security!

*He tiptoes towards possible heavy objects. Tries his shoe as a cosh
. . . hopeless. Picks up his keys, makes them into a knuckle-duster.
Hopeless. There is a sound of wind from off.*

John Mother!!!!

Picks up a pot plant. Holds it by plant, pot as the hammer part.
Fylgia *advances towards him.*

John Ooooh!
I've got no money!

Cashpoint were empty!
I've no jewellery, I'm a divorced man!
Look at the time!
My brother's due back from Judo Training any
minute . . .

The **Fylgia** *stands.*

John   Have you escaped from somewhere high
security?
Only I could ring for an ambul . . .

The **Fylgia** *holds out its hand.* **John** *shrinks back.* **Fylgia**
hands him a handful of sleeping pills. Then a party cracker.

John   Oh.
Are you from next door?
The Flats?
Are you from the Party?

Fylgia *smiles.*

John   You want me to pull the cracker?
Swallow these?
All right . . . then I must love you and leave you I've
got Karate Training first thing . . .

They pull the cracker.

Well, there's a hat and a pocket nail-clipper . . .
which do you . . . ?
I'll put on the hat, shall I . . .
and this is for you . . .
(*He touches the* **Fylgia**'s *hand.*) Who are you?

Thirty-six: Ghost

Joy's *flat. A* **Fylgia** *sits in her chair. It has a glass of*
champagne and is drinking it. **Joy** *is heard off.*

Joy   Oh God!
Oh Jesus!

Oh Jesus, Mary and Joseph!
Where's the bloody garlic?
Bloody onions!
Ah!
Ahah!
Here we go!!!!

She enters. She has a bible, a makeshift cross and a string of garlic.

Joy   All right!
I'm a Christian!
All my family are Catholics and I've been confirmed.
Now Go Away!!!!

She points her artefacts at the **Fylgia**. *It drinks.*

I blame Hollywood for this!
Making ghosts acceptable!
This is a new designer condominium complex!
It shouldn't be haunted! (*She puts the stuff down.*)
All right, let's start again.
Did you meet with an untimely death?
Did someone murder you brutally and you want me to
get in touch with the authorities?

Fylgia *listens.*

Joy   Are you desperately unhappy on the other side?

Fylgia *shakes its head.*

Joy   Do you want me to contact *Psychic News* and put
an advert in for a loved one?

Fylgia *shakes its head.*

Joy   But you want to get in touch with someone?

It nods its head.

Who?

Fylgia *leans forward. Opens its mouth.*

Yes?
Can you communicate?
Yes?
Who do you want to get in touch with?

Fylgia *reaches out its hand. It points to* **Joy**.

Me.
Me?

Thirty-seven: *National Geographic*

John's *room.* **John** *and* **Fylgia** *looking at photographs.*

John   You see that's me in my cricketing whites!
Playing for my school!
Wheelston Boys, Cheadle.
D'you know it?
Are you from round here?
This is me on *The Regal Lady*.
That's Scarborough.
Do you know Scarborough?
Morecambe?
Blackpool?
I've got some of me . . .

Fylgia *looks away, mildly bored.*

John   You see if you could give me a clue . . . we
could ring a taxi and . . .

Fylgia *picks up a magazine. It is the* National
Geographic.

Yes, that's my Geography Magaz . . .
But we don't want to . . .
All right, we'll have a look at . . .
The Antarctic . . .

Fylgia *smiles.*

John   Well, I've never been there . . .

Have you?
No!
Yes?

Fylgia *turns the pages.*

John It's melting you know . . .
oh, Uruguayan humming-bird . . .
Yes, that's rain forest.
They're chopping all that down of course.

Fylgia *knows all this.*

John That's the Pacific Ocean.
Fished Out.
It's like Washing-Up Water.
Ah, Galapagos Islands.
All these animals are on the endangered Species List
look . . .
Desert. Egypt.
With this Greenhouse Effect Palaver it's all going to be
Desert soon.
All of it.
We've ruined and wrecked it.
Wiped Out.

He looks at the **Fylgia**.

Oh My Goodness!

Thirty-eight: A party game

Joy's *room.* **Fylgia** *still sitting.* **Joy** *lying in its lap.*

Joy So you're not a ghost?
Right.
And you're not a rapist . . .
A Jehovah's Witness
or somebody come to steal my CD . . .
You've got to tell me when I'm getting warm . . .
Are you a space creature from a higher intelligence than

our own come to aid humanity and save it from itself?
No.
Are you a space creature from a *lower* intelligence than
our own come to ... No.
Are you a prototype humanoid that *Which* magazine
have sent to selected high-class consumers to sort of ...
road test?
No.
Are you a strangely fascinating dream that I'm going to
wake up from?
Are you from a parallel world?
Are you a figment of my imagination?
Are you a throwback experience from when I used to
drop acid?
Am I anywhere near warm?
No.
You said you wanted to contact me.
Why me?
Am I special?
I'm not.
I'm ever so ordinary.
Millions like me.
Millions.
Tell me.
Please.
I want to know.

Thirty-nine: A long sleep

Miriam's *room. The* **Fylgia** *is waiting.* **Miriam** *comes in
ready for bed.*

Miriam   Right, that's all locked up.
All safe and sound.
Snug as a bug in a rug.
Now then ... time for off.

Fylgia *takes her in its arms. Music ...* 'Nothing Compares

To U'.

Miriam   Oh, I say.
I haven't done this since Jack and me were members of
Darby and Joan!

They dance.

We were third in the Veleeta!
We used to love to dance.
Both of us.
I were better on accuracy of steps . . .
but he had more style!
Just like Fred Astaire and Ginger Rogers!
My daughter Rachel can't dance.
But I still love her.

They dance. The **Fylgia** *puts its hand gently over her face. She
dances slower and slower. She stops and slumps.* **Fylgia** *carries
her gently off. She is not breathing.*

Forty: In dreams

John*'s room. He is swallowing pills.* **Fylgia** *attends.*

John   Half of me's always wanted to go to those places.
But you've been.
I've always felt I knew them though.
But I was always afraid they'd be dirty
or smaller
or not bright colours
or disappointing.
Like here.
Half of me was always afraid of that.
So I stayed put.
Put up with it.
Settled for less.
And that's what I got.
Less.
Half of me's always known that.

Only half of me's been anywhere!
I didn't cut the Metro in half.
I drove it to Heathrow.
See her and 'Tony' off.
Maybe sneak some rotting fish into their luggage!
Eilat Beach Hotel . . . let's unpack
Poooooghhhh!!!!
They looked that damn happy!
I ran to Short Stay Level Four.
Metro . . . off!
Half me mind still on her . . . loving . . . face.

Fylgia *puts its arm round* **John**.

John   I clipped a Nissan Micra.
It . . . spun . . . across two lanes.
I drove on.
I think something happened.
This is committing suicide, in't it?

They hug. **John** *goes limp and when* **Fylgia** *extricates itself from his arms,* **John** *does not move.* **Fylgia** *takes off* **John**'s *party hat and leaves.*

Forty-one: Ten reasons to live

Lily's *room.* **Rachel** *emerges from the bedroom. She is looking for various articles of her clothing. As she searches, she comes to the music. Puts it on. Sinead O'Connor: 'I Do Not Want What I Haven't Got'. As the music starts, light rises on* **Joy**'s *room.* **Joy** *is looking at the* **Fylgia**.

Rachel (*putting on her footwear as* **Lily** *enters*)   Ten reasons to be happy you're alive.

Lily   What a mistake, hey?

Rachel   One. You can make mistakes.

Fylgia *locks hold of* **Joy**.

Lily (*to music*)   . . . Oh . . . (*Goes to music.*)
I hate this game.

Rachel   Two. Music.

Lily (*shutting off music. To it*)   . . . Shut the fuck up!

Rachel   Three. Freedom of choice.

Joy *tries to throw the* **Fylgia** *off. It resists her.*

Lily   I fucking hate Sinead O'Connor.

Rachel   Four. Strong emotions!

Lily   I'm sorry. Last night. I don't think . . .

Rachel   Five. (*Takes her hands.*) Human contact.

Joy *and* **Fylgia** *struggle.*

Lily   I miss her.

Rachel (*puts her arms round her*)   Six. Love.

Lily *cries.*

Joy *is on her hands and knees, dry vomiting, the* **Fylgia** *near.*

Rachel   Seven. Time.
Eight. Friends.
Hey, I think your friend Helen is very nice indeed.
Why don't you . . .
I'd better go. (*She goes to the door.*)
Nine. Fresh new days.
Ten. Telephones. You got my number.
You know what the Reverend Mother says . . .

Lily   'When one door closes,
another door slams shut in your face.'

Rachel   Now, that's *not* what the Reverend Mother
says . . .

She exits.

Joy   Oh Jesus!

I'm drowning in my own Sick!!!!

Lights out on **Joy**.

Lily *rises, walks to* **Helen** *who is standing waiting, at her door.*

Lily   I slept with Rachel.

Helen   I hate you.

Lily   I miss Mary.

Helen   I'm sick to death of hearing about Mary.
You're so stupid.
You're so stupid!

Lily   I haven't been thinking straight.

Helen   I'm fed up of looking after you.

Lily   I've got a great hole in my chest.
My head's fibreglass.
I'm all over the place.

Helen   Good!

Lily   I want you to wait around for me.

Helen   Why? I did. Have.

Lily   Till it fills up. My chest.
Then I want us to fall in love and live happily ever after.

Helen (*pause. Sighs. Furious*)   Well, I've done my half of that actually . . .

Lily   I'll do my half.
I just need a bit of time.

Helen   No looking after!

Lily   No!
(*Pause.*) Well, just a little . . .

Helen *takes her hand.* **Mary** *and* **Fylgias** *watch as they exit.*

Mary (*alight with the complete energy of complete
realisation*) Dying yes yes yes!!!
You end you end you end
We just die because we just die
simple as that simple . . .

One **Fylgia** *disappears theatrically, magically.*

Mary Nothing more.

Another disappears.

Mary Nothing after.

Another. They are all gone.

Mary Oh oh oh
I want Joy!
Pure, present joy!
Now!
Now!
Now!

The abyss gapes. The **Fylgias** *are revealed above, playing cards.*
Mary *lies back in her wreckage. Sinead O'Connor sings the last
verse of 'Nothing Compares To U'.*

Lightning Source UK Ltd.
Milton Keynes UK
02 March 2011

168541UK00001B/7/P